Who Gets Your Passwords?

TheSeniorTechie Guide To Digital Estate Planning

Paul Wilczynski
TheSeniorTechie

Published in the United States of America
First Edition, 2026

Paperback ISBN: 979-8-9955017-2-5
Digital ISBN: 979-8-9955017-3-2
Library of Congress Control Number: 2026915297

Published by TheSeniorTechie Press
TheSeniorTechiePress.com

Disclaimer: This book is intended for informational purposes only and does not constitute legal, financial, or professional advice. Readers should consult qualified professionals for guidance specific to their circumstances.

Interior design by Andrea Kulish Wilhelm/Studio A

Front cover design concept by Paul Wilczynski;
imagery created with assistance from generative tools.

Illustration credits: p. 1 shafiuzzaman/stock.adobe.com;
p. 21 Rupali/stock.adobe.com;
p. 43 + 139 AbbasyKautsar/stock.adobe.com;
p. 61 vectorsanta/stock.adobe.com;
p. 77 blankstock/stock.adobe.com;
p. 95 woopicx.com/stock.adobe.com;
p. 121 Vectuz/stock.adobe.com;
p. 161 Andrea Kulish Wilhelm and Cetacons/stock.adobe.com

Who Gets Your Passwords?

TheSeniorTechie Guide To Digital Estate Planning

TABLE OF CONTENTS

1—What Is Your Digital Estate and Why It Matters.....1

2—Your Digital Account Inventory: No Spreadsheet Degree Required.....21

3—Passwords, Access, and Who Gets In When You Can't...43

4—Don't Let Your Lifetime of Photos Disappear.....61

5—What Happens to Your Social Media When You Die?...77

6—The Financial Freeze: Keeping Your Money Accessible When You Can't.....95

7—The Conversation: How to Tell Your Family What You've Done.....121

8—The "For My Family" Package: Bringing It All Together ..139

A Few Terms Worth Knowing.....157

About the Author.....161

About the Designer and the Type.....163

CHAPTER ONE

WHAT IS YOUR DIGITAL ESTATE AND WHY IT MATTERS

The part of your life that lives on a screen, and what happens to it when you can't protect it yourself

Carol didn't think of herself as someone who couldn't handle things. She had handled plenty. She had buried her mother, settled her father's estate, raised three kids mostly on her own after her divorce, and built a small accounting practice from scratch. When her husband Richard died on a morning in March, she was heartbroken, but she was not helpless.

Except when it came to the iPad.

Richard had kept everything on that iPad. Recipes he'd collected for twenty years. Fishing logs going back to the 1990s. Thousands of photographs, including almost every picture taken at their grandchildren's birthdays. He had also used it to manage a small brokerage account he'd set up on his own, the kind of thing he was proud of and slightly secretive about in the way men of his generation sometimes were with money.

Carol knew the iPad existed. She did not know the passcode. She called Apple. They were polite and sorry for her loss and absolutely unable to help without documentation she didn't have and a legal process she hadn't started. Eight months later, she had recovered the brokerage account through the firm's own procedures. The photographs are still on that iPad. The iPad still sits in the drawer of Richard's nightstand. She can't bring herself to throw it away, and she can't get into it, and that particular kind of loss, she told me, is different from the other kinds. It sits there every night, three feet from where she sleeps, and she can't reach it.

That's what this book is about.

I wrote this so you could pick it up anywhere. Some topics come up in more than one chapter because the issues overlap in real life, and I didn't want any chapter to leave you stranded if you skipped the one before it. If something feels familiar, that's intentional, not an accident.

The Part of Your Estate That's Completely Unprotected

When most people hear the word "estate," they think of a will. Maybe a trust. A list of who gets the furniture and who gets the grandmother's china. If they're thorough, they've named beneficiaries on their retirement accounts and life insurance policies. That's the traditional infrastructure of leaving your life in order, and it matters enormously.

But there's a second layer now, one that didn't exist a generation ago, and most estate plans don't touch it at all. It's the part of your life that lives on a screen. Your email. Your bank's website. Your photos in the cloud. Your subscriptions. Your social media. Your passwords. Your devices.

All of that is your digital estate, and for most people reading this book, it's completely unprotected.

Not unprotected in a legal sense, necessarily. Unprotected

in the practical sense. Unprotected in the sense that if something happens to you tomorrow, the people you love most would have almost no way to access any of it without enormous effort, legal intervention, or plain luck. And some of it they might never reach at all.

That's not a scare tactic. That's just how these systems were designed. They were designed to protect you while you're alive. Nobody thought very hard, at least not until recently, about what happens when you're not.

What Counts as a Digital Asset

Before you can plan for something, you have to know what you're planning for. So let's get specific.

A digital asset is any account, file, or piece of data that exists online or on a device. That definition sounds simple until you start making a real list, at which point most people discover they have significantly more than they realized.

Start with email. It's a digital asset, and often the master key to every other account you own online.

Online banking comes next. Almost every bank now has a web portal, and most people use it at least occasionally to check balances or pay bills. If you bank with more than one institution, you may have two or three of these. Investment accounts are the same. So are accounts at credit unions, online-only banks, or apps like Venmo or PayPal that you might use to send money to grandchildren.

Social media is next, and people are often surprised by how many platforms they're on. Facebook is the obvious one for this age group, but there's also Instagram if you've been talked into it, YouTube if you watch it regularly enough to have created an account, LinkedIn if you're still professionally active or ever were, and Pinterest if you've spent any time collecting recipes or garden ideas. Each of those is a separate account with a separate password.

Then there are photo libraries. This is the category that tends to hit people hardest emotionally. If you have an iPhone or iPad, your photos are almost certainly backed up to iCloud whether you set that up intentionally or not. Android users are probably backed up to Google Photos. Amazon offers its own photo storage to Prime members. Some people have their photos spread across two or three of these services without realizing it. The pictures of your children as babies, your parents who are gone, your wedding, your grandchildren's first steps, every birthday party and holiday and unremarkable afternoon that someone thought to photograph, all of it lives in these services. And without the right credentials and a plan, your family may have real trouble reaching any of it.

Subscriptions round out the obvious picture. Netflix, Hulu, Amazon Prime. The newspaper you read online. The magazine app. The music service. None of these are sentimental, but they are financial. If a subscription is charged to a credit card that your family doesn't know about, and the card stays active after you're gone, those charges keep coming. It's not catastrophic, but it's one more unnecessary complication in an already complicated time.

The Assets You're Probably Not Thinking About

Then there are the ones people almost never think about until someone points them out.

Airline miles, hotel points, and credit card rewards balances can represent real money, and Chapter Two covers how to make sure they're included in your account inventory.

Digital purchases are another category worth naming. If

you've bought movies or books through Amazon, Apple, or Google, you have a library that lives in those accounts. Strictly speaking, you don't own most of that content the way you own a physical book or DVD. You've purchased a license to watch or read it, and what happens to that license when you die is governed by each company's terms of service, not by your will. It's worth being honest with your family about what those libraries are, even if the legal question of who inherits them is murky.

And finally, your devices themselves. Your phone, your tablet, your laptop, your desktop computer. This is the physical gateway to almost everything else. Every app you use, every account you stay logged into, every saved password that fills in automatically when you visit a website, all of it runs through your devices. If your family can't unlock your phone, they lose access not just to what's on the phone but to the easiest path into everything connected to it. The device isn't just a tool. It's the front door.

Add it up honestly and most people are looking at more accounts than they'd guess. The average person now manages well over a hundred passwords, according to recent research, and while not every password represents a separate account that matters, the sheer volume surprises almost everyone who actually sits down to count.

If you have already set up online banking, named a beneficiary on a retirement account, or made sure a family member knows your phone passcode, you are further along than most people who open this book, and that matters. Those are not small things. That is a foundation.

What follows is not a mandate to rebuild everything from scratch. It is a way to see what you have, find the gaps, and close them one at a time. Nobody does all of this in a weekend, and nobody needs to. The goal is a plan that is good enough to protect the people you love, not a perfect document that required six months of your life to produce. Good enough, built steadily, is exactly what this book is designed to help you reach.

Dorothy's Inbox

Dorothy had been widowed for three years when her daughter Karen finally convinced her to sit down and make a list of her own accounts. They did it at the kitchen table on a Saturday afternoon, which is how these conversations tend to happen, informally and a little reluctantly, over coffee.

They got to twenty-six accounts before Dorothy started feeling tired and they agreed to take a break. What surprised them both wasn't the number. It was how many accounts Dorothy used regularly but couldn't quite remember the passwords for, relying instead on her browser to fill them in automatically. She knew her email password. She knew her bank password. For at least a dozen other accounts, she said, she honestly had no idea. The browser just does it.

That's not unusual. It's actually the norm. The convenience features built into modern browsers and phones are so good at remembering passwords that most people stop remembering them personally. Which is completely fine while you're alive and using your own devices. It becomes a serious problem when someone else needs access.

Karen's concern wasn't morbid, and she said so. "Mom, I'm not planning for you to die tomorrow. I just want to know where things are." That's the right framing, and it's worth holding onto as you read this book. This isn't planning for death. It's planning for continuity, for the reasonable likelihood that at some point, someone you trust is going to need to know what you have and how to reach it.

What Actually Happens Without a Plan

The honest answer is: it depends, and most of the outcomes aren't good.

When someone dies, their family typically has two problems. The first is access. They need to get into accounts to manage, close, or transfer them. The second is knowledge. They need to know the accounts exist in the first place.

Access is the problem most people think about, but knowledge is often harder. A forgotten savings account at an online bank, a small investment portfolio managed through an app, a PayPal balance that never got moved to a checking account, a digital gift card balance, a rewards program worth real money. None of these appear in a traditional estate inventory because none of them were on the traditional estate planning radar. They just sit there, undiscovered, until eventually the institution turns the unclaimed funds over to the state.

The scale of this problem is larger than most people realize. State treasurers across the country are currently holding an estimated seventy billion dollars in unclaimed property, according to the National Association of Unclaimed Property Administrators, with roughly one in seven Americans owed some portion of it. Much of that represents accounts people simply forgot to tell their families about, or accounts their families couldn't find because there was no record of them.

The access problem is more immediately frustrating. Each platform handles death differently, and none of them make it particularly easy.

This Isn't Only About Dying

Most people, when they hear the phrase "digital estate

planning," picture a will. They picture death. That's understandable, because that's what the word "estate" usually signals. But a significant number of the situations that send families scrambling for digital access have nothing to do with dying. They involve incapacity, and in some ways those situations are harder.

A stroke. A cancer diagnosis that requires weeks of treatment and recovery. A bad fall that sends someone to a rehabilitation facility for two months. A serious infection that puts an otherwise healthy person in the hospital for three weeks. These are the events that arrive without warning and hand the people who love you an immediate, practical problem: the accounts still exist, the bills are still running, and you cannot manage any of it yourself right now.

Consider what happened to a retired teacher named Miriam. She had a minor stroke in her mid-seventies, spent three weeks in the hospital and another five weeks in a short-term rehabilitation facility before coming home. Her daughter moved in to help during recovery. At some point in that first week back, they discovered that two automatic bill payments had missed because the linked checking account had been frozen after Miriam's bank flagged the absence of activity. A streaming subscription had quietly lapsed. And one account, a longtime email address Miriam used to stay in touch with a book club, had been locked out entirely after a family member tried three times with wrong passwords trying to be helpful. The account recovery process required a verification code sent to a backup phone number that was no longer in service.

Miriam recovered. Which meant she got to deal with the cleanup herself once she was back on her feet. But the experience shook her, because she realized that the disorganization she had always planned to address "eventually" had just caused real problems during the eight weeks she needed her accounts to simply keep running without her.

The incapacity scenario is harder than the death scenario in at least one specific way. When someone has died, there is a clear legal status and a clear direction of travel. When someone is incapacitated but alive, the rules get murkier. The person still owns the accounts. They may be capable of approving decisions but unable to execute them. A family member acting in good faith to keep the lights on can end up inadvertently triggering security flags, locking accounts further, or doing things the account holder, once recovered, wishes had been done differently.

Everything this book describes, the inventory, the access plan, the family conversation, works equally well for incapacity as it does for death. Think of it not as preparation for a final event, but as preparation for any moment when someone you trust needs to step in. That framing changes nothing about what you actually do. It changes how it feels to do it.

The Gap Nobody Mentions

Most people who have done any estate planning at all have a will. Some have a trust, a durable power of attorney, a healthcare directive. They worked with an attorney, or used an online service, or updated documents after a major life event. They feel reasonably confident that they have taken care of things.

Those documents almost certainly do not address digital accounts. Not because the attorney made a mistake, and not because you forgot to ask. It's because this category of asset either didn't exist when many of these documents were written, or because neither party thought to raise it. Estate planning as a profession developed over decades when the assets that needed transferring were physical: real property, financial accounts held at institutions, jewelry, vehicles, personal belongings. The frameworks that attorneys use, the language that powers of attorney traditionally employ, the categories that wills move through, were built for that world.

The result, for most families, is a plan that covers the house and the bank accounts and the grandmother's china, but leaves the family with no legal authority and no practical guidance for the email account, the photo library, the social media profiles, the streaming subscriptions, and the password-protected devices that now hold the practical keys to almost everything else.

The gap exists on both sides of the conversation. Most clients don't raise digital accounts because it doesn't occur to them that estate planning should cover those things. Most attorneys don't raise it proactively because they are following their clients' lead, focused on the issues the clients bring in, and digital assets remain, for many practices, a specialty concern rather than a standard part of every engagement. The subject simply falls through the space between.

Here is the practical consequence: even if you have a perfectly valid durable power of attorney that authorizes someone to manage your financial affairs while you're alive and incapacitated, that document may not give your agent the authority to access your digital accounts. Most platform terms of service do not recognize powers of attorney. The legal authority that works at your bank does not automatically translate to authority recognized by the company that runs your email or your photo storage. Whether and how a power of attorney covers digital accounts depends on how it's written and what it specifically addresses. It's worth asking an attorney about, particularly if your documents are more than a few years old.

None of this is a reason to panic or to redo your entire estate plan. It is a reason to understand the gap, and to take practical steps that don't require an attorney at all: the account inventory, the access plan, the conversation with your family about where things are. Those steps do more to protect your family than any legal document, because they work at the practical level, where most of the problems actually happen.

If you have an attorney you trust, add digital accounts to your next conversation with them. But don't wait for that conversation to start the rest of this book.

You Don't Own What You Think You Own

Here is something most people find genuinely surprising when they first hear it: the email account you've had for twenty years is not yours in the way your car is yours. Neither is your Facebook profile. Neither is the digital library of movies you've bought through Amazon, or the collection of albums in your Apple Music account, or the books in your Kindle library. You have not purchased those things. You have purchased a license to use them, under terms set by each company, and those terms can restrict what happens to the account when the license holder dies.

The terms of service agreements you clicked through when you created these accounts, the ones that are thousands of words long and that essentially nobody reads, typically specify that the account belongs to the individual who created it and cannot be transferred. The account does not become part of your estate in the traditional sense. It continues to exist as a separate legal entity, governed by the platform's policies, and those policies were not written with your heirs in mind.

This is not a legal technicality designed to frustrate families. It's the architecture of how the internet was built, by companies whose primary concern was protecting the privacy of their living users, who reasonably enough didn't want their email read by strangers. The same security that protects you from hackers makes it genuinely difficult for your family to access your accounts after you're gone, even when their motives are entirely legitimate.

The practical implication is this: the fact that you spent years building a digital library, maintaining an account, accumulating content, does not create a right your family can simply step into. What creates that right is the tools the platforms themselves offer, the designated contacts, the legacy settings, the inactive account managers, all of which you have to set up while you are alive and able to do so. Once you're gone, that window closes. The platform's terms of service, whatever they say, are what your family is left with.

This is not a reason for despair, and it's not a reason to stop using these services. It is a specific, practical argument for using the tools the platforms already provide, before you need them. Apple's Legacy Contact feature. Google's Inactive Account Manager. The emergency access features built into password managers. Facebook's memorialization settings. These are not complicated. They take minutes to set up. And they are the difference between your family having a clear path to what you've left behind and your family spending months trying to get a company's customer service to recognize a situation those policies weren't designed to handle. The chapters that follow are going to walk you through exactly how to use them.

How the Big Platforms Handle It

Apple is strict: without a passcode or Apple ID credentials, a family faces months of legal documentation to recover an account, and sometimes the process fails entirely. Apple does offer a Legacy Contact feature that lets you designate someone in advance, and Chapter Three walks through exactly how to set it up.

Google offers a similar tool called Inactive Account Manager, which lets you designate trusted contacts who can access your data if your account goes dormant. Chapter Three covers that setup as well.

Facebook lets you designate a Legacy Contact to manage your profile in a limited way after you die; without one, Facebook's default is to memorialize the account. Chapter Five covers what that means and how to set your own preferences before it becomes someone else's problem.

Each platform has its own policies, its own processes, and its own gaps. And the policies change. What's true today may be different in two years. The only thing that stays constant is this: planning ahead while you're alive puts you in control. Leaving it to chance puts your family at the mercy of whatever each company's current policy happens to be.

The Things You've Created That Nobody Knows About

There's a category of digital assets that's harder to describe but just as important, and it's the one that tends to make people feel something when they think about it honestly.

It's everything you've written, collected, or created.

The emails you've sent over twenty years. Not the utility notices and the promotional offers, but the real ones, the messages to your children during hard times, the correspondence with friends who are gone, the thread with your sister that stretches back to whenever you both first got email. Most of us have written things in email that we'd never write on paper, things that are frank and funny and real, and they exist somewhere in a server farm in a data center, and most families never get to them.

The journals some people keep in apps like Day One or even in Google Docs. The genealogy research that took years and lives in an Ancestry.com account. The creative projects, the novel someone has been working on quietly, the photography portfolio, the collection of recipes in a digital file that was meant to become a family cookbook someday.

Barbara had kept a journal for thirty-one years.

Not a diary in the teenage sense, nothing with a lock and a ribbon. It was more like a running record of her life, observations about her garden, notes from the books she was reading, letters she wrote to her mother after her mother developed dementia and could no longer really receive them. She kept it in a private blog she'd started sometime around 2005, back when blogs were something people did. It wasn't public. Nobody read it. It was just hers.

When Barbara had a stroke at seventy-eight, her daughter Ellen came to stay with her during recovery. At some point Ellen asked about the journal, which Barbara had mentioned over the years in the vague way people mention things they consider private. Barbara could remember the name of the site. She could not remember the password. She could not remember the email address she'd used to create the account, which had been a work address from a job she'd left fifteen years earlier.

Barbara recovered well enough to manage on her own again. But she and Ellen spent three weeks trying to get back into that account, and they never did. Thirty-one years of writing. Gone, as far as either of them could reach it, not because Barbara died, but because she got sick for six weeks and couldn't manage her own login.

That's the part people don't always think about. This isn't only a plan for dying. It's a plan for the moment when something happens and someone you love needs to find what matters to you.

None of this has obvious financial value. All of it has meaning. And right now, for most people, all of it is at risk of simply disappearing.

That's not melodrama. Platforms shut down. Accounts get deleted when they're considered inactive. Google has stated outright that it reserves the right to delete accounts that have been dormant for two years. If nobody knows something exists, nobody can fight to preserve it. Planning for your digital estate isn't just about money and accounts. It's about deciding what matters and making sure it can be found.

Gerald's Project

Gerald spent eleven years building a genealogy record for his family. He started because his mother had mentioned, once, that there might be some Cherokee ancestry on her father's side, and he wanted to know if it was true. Eleven years later he had documentation going back five generations on three branches of the family, had connected with cousins he'd never known existed, and had put together a record that his children and grandchildren would genuinely want to have someday.

The whole thing lived in his Ancestry.com account. His subscription auto-renewed every year on a credit card. He had mentioned it to his wife in passing but never shown her how to access it, where the account was, or what the login information was. He had a folder on his computer labeled "Family History" but it hadn't been updated in two years, and his wife wasn't sure if the current version of the research was on the computer or only online.

Gerald isn't gone. He's seventy-three, healthy, and still adding to the project. But his daughter, who read an earlier version of this chapter, pointed it out to him directly. "Dad, if something happened to you tomorrow, I wouldn't know where any of this was." He hadn't thought about it that way. He thought of the project as something he was doing, not something he was leaving behind.

Most of us are the same way. We're in the middle of our lives. We're not thinking about the ending. But the things we're creating and collecting and corresponding about are accumulating every day, and at some point someone else is going to need to know they exist.

Why "My Family Will Figure It Out" Doesn't Work

This is the most common alternative plan, and it's worth taking apart briefly because it sounds more reasonable than it is.

The logic goes like this: my kids are smart, they know I bank online, they'll find the accounts, they'll call customer service, they'll sort it out. And it's true that families do sometimes sort it out. But sorting it out in the absence of any preparation typically means months of work, significant stress during an already difficult time, and real losses along the way.

Customer service at most financial institutions requires account verification that only the account holder can typically provide. Calling to say "my father had an account here, can you tell me what's in it" produces a polite refusal in most cases. The legal mechanisms exist to eventually compel disclosure, but they require probate proceedings, legal documentation, and time that most families don't want to spend in the months after losing someone.

Passwords are a particular problem. Modern security is designed to prevent unauthorized access, which is exactly what a grieving family member looks like to a computer system. Wrong password too many times and accounts lock. Account recovery processes route through email and phone numbers that may no longer be accessible. Two-factor authentication sends codes to a phone the family can't unlock.

None of this is the platform's fault. They built these systems to protect you. The problem is that protection doesn't automatically transfer to the people you trust most. You have to set that up yourself.

The good news, and there is substantial good news, is that setting it up is genuinely not complicated. The rest of this book is going to walk you through exactly what to do, in plain language, at a pace that won't overwhelm you. You don't need technical expertise. You don't need a lawyer to get started. You need a willingness to spend a few hours over the coming weeks doing something that your family will be quietly grateful for for the rest of their lives, even if they never quite say so.

What This Book Will Cover

Each chapter covers a distinct piece of the picture—inventory, passwords and access, photos, social media, financial accounts, the family conversation, and bringing it all together. The chapters build on each other, but you don't have to read them in order. If you know exactly what you're worried about, start there. Each chapter is designed to stand on its own.

The Real Reason to Do This

Carol eventually got the brokerage account sorted out. The financial piece resolved itself through official channels, which is how financial accounts usually go, slowly and with paperwork, but they get there. It was the photographs she couldn't get back.

She knew what was on that iPad. She could list the pictures she remembered, the ones she'd watched Richard take, the ones she'd been in. Knowing they existed but being unable to reach them turned out to be worse, in some ways, than if they'd been lost in a fire. Something lost in a fire is gone. Something locked in a drawer three feet from where you sleep every night is a different kind of absence.

Planning your digital estate is not a legal exercise, though it touches legal questions. It is not primarily a financial exercise, though it has real financial consequences. At its core, it's an act of consideration. It's saying to the people who will outlive you: I thought about what you'd need, and I made it as easy as I could.

That's worth a few hours of your time. Let's get started.

What To Do This Week

The first task is simply to make a list. Not a complete inventory, not yet. Just sit down for fifteen minutes and write down every online account you can think of off the top of your head. Your email. Your bank. Your social media. Your photo storage. Your streaming services. Don't worry about passwords or what to do with the list. Just get it on paper. Most people are surprised by how many things surface even in a quick pass, and the act of writing them down is the beginning of having a plan.

The second task is to check whether you have a Legacy

Contact set up with Apple or a similar designation with Google, if you use either of those platforms. You don't need to configure anything this week. Just confirm whether it's been done. Chapter Three will walk you through the full setup when you're ready.

The third task is to tell one person that you're working on this. It doesn't have to be a formal conversation. It can be as simple as mentioning to your spouse, your adult child, or a close friend that you've been thinking about getting your digital accounts organized. That small acknowledgment makes you more likely to follow through, and it opens the door to a conversation that most families need to have but rarely start.

The fourth task is to find the passcode for one device you use regularly, confirm that someone you trust knows it, or make a note of it somewhere that person could find. Not a sticky note on the device, but somewhere considered, a piece of paper in an envelope, a note in a file you'll show them. One device. One passcode. That's a week's worth of progress, and it's more than most people have done.

CHAPTER TWO

YOUR DIGITAL ACCOUNT INVENTORY: NO SPREADSHEET DEGREE REQUIRED

You don't need to organize everything at once—just start with knowing what you have and where it lives.

A few years ago I sat down on a Sunday afternoon to count how many online accounts I had. I figured it would take twenty minutes.

It took three hours. I filled most of a legal pad. And when I was done, I was fairly certain I'd still missed some.

Not because my life is complicated. Because I'd been signing up for things online for twenty-plus years and had never once stopped to count. An email account here. Online banking there. A photo backup service I set up when I got a new phone. A genealogy site my sister talked me into. A streaming service I forgot to cancel. None of it felt like "building a digital estate" when I was doing it. It felt like ordinary life.

But it adds up. Research by Bryn Mawr Trust found that the average American now has up to 250 digital accounts. Not 25. Two hundred and fifty. Separate research on password habits puts the average number of passwords a person manages at around 120. Your number is probably somewhere in that range, and I'd bet real money you couldn't name half of them right now without help.

That's not a memory problem. That's just the reality of how we've all been living online for the past two decades.

Why Your Family Can't Figure It Out After the Fact

In a 2024 survey of 1,500 U.S. adults conducted by Bryn Mawr Trust, respondents were asked to estimate the value of everything they store and manage online. The average answer came back at $191,516. That figure blends things with a clear dollar value, like bank accounts and investment portfolios managed online, with things whose value is harder to quantify but no less real, like thirty years of family photographs or an email archive that no one else could reconstruct. The point isn't that your photos have a precise market price. The point is that when people actually stop and think about what they'd lose, the number gets big fast. And fewer than 15% of Americans have any kind of estate plan that addresses those assets at all.

That gap between what we have and what we've planned for is the entire problem this chapter exists to solve.

The families who end up in trouble aren't the ones whose loved ones had complicated digital lives. They're the ones whose loved ones had ordinary digital lives, exactly like yours and mine, and simply never made a list. They left behind no map. A survey of professional inheritance advisers found that nearly a quarter had clients who experienced serious difficulties accessing a deceased family member's digital accounts. Not minor inconvenience. Real distress. And 90% of those advisers expected the problem to grow in the years ahead.

Picture what that actually looks like. A son sits down at

his father's laptop the week after the funeral. He knows his father banked somewhere, paid bills online, had a few streaming services, and kept in touch with old friends on Facebook. He doesn't know the email address his father used for most of his accounts. He doesn't know whether there's one email address or three. He doesn't know which bank, because his father always just called it "the bank." He doesn't know the laptop's password, and when he calls the bank to explain the situation, they tell him they can't discuss the account without proper legal documentation, which will take several weeks to obtain.

He's not dealing with a complicated estate. He's dealing with an ordinary one. The problem isn't the accounts. The problem is that nobody wrote anything down.

This is a solvable problem. A list won't solve everything, but it's where everything starts.

The Particular Problem of "I Know Where Everything Is"

Evelyn had been managing the household finances for forty years. She knew every bank account, every insurance policy, every investment. When her husband Frank passed away, she wasn't worried about the money. She knew exactly where it was.

What she didn't know was that Frank had been paying for six separate subscriptions on his personal credit card, two of them on autopay that kept charging after his death. She didn't know that his email had become the catch-all for account alerts from three financial institutions, landing in an inbox she couldn't access. She didn't know about the PayPal account he'd set up years earlier, linked to an old checking account she'd already closed.

None of this was secret. Frank wasn't hiding anything. He just hadn't thought to explain it, because it all made sense to him and he figured he'd have time to sort it out eventually.

He didn't. Most of us don't.

The promise you're making to your family by building this inventory isn't "here are my passwords." It's "here is a map of my digital life, so that if something happens to me, you're not starting from zero." That's an act of care that takes one afternoon.

What You're Actually Building

Before we get into the how, it's worth being clear about what this inventory actually is, because people sometimes overcomplicate it in their heads.

You are not building a password document. Passwords come later, in a different place, handled differently.

You are not writing a legal document. No lawyers required.

You are building a simple list that answers one question: what accounts do I have and where do they live? That's it. Think of it as a map. Not a set of keys. Just a map.

For each account on the list, you only need to capture four things. The name of the service. What it's for. Roughly where the login information lives. And whether it has a recurring charge attached to it.

That's the whole format. Name, purpose, where to find the login, and whether money is moving through it. A single line per account, or a short block of four lines. Nothing more complicated than that.

To make that concrete, here is what three entries might actually look like on your list:

Gmail, personal email, login info in the small black notebook in the desk drawer, no recurring charge.

Chase Bank, checking and savings, login info in the same notebook, autopay for electric bill and Netflix.

iCloud, iPhone backup and photos, login is my Apple ID, stored in the notebook, monthly fee on Visa ending in 4471.

That's it. Three lines, or three short blocks, and anyone who needs to find those accounts can do so without guessing. You are not writing instructions. You are leaving a trail of breadcrumbs. The person who comes after you doesn't need a manual. They need to know where to look.

Day Zero: Before the Week Starts

Before you begin the actual inventory work, there's a preparation step worth doing. Think of it as day zero. It's not part of the seven-day plan. It's what you do the evening before you start, or on a weekend afternoon, to make the week easier.

It has two parts, and together they take about twenty minutes.

The first part is an inbox search. Go to your main email account and search for each of these phrases, one at a time: "welcome," "verify your email," "thanks for signing up," and "confirm your account." Run each search and scroll through what comes up. You will find accounts you have completely forgotten about. This is not because you're disorganized. It's because you signed up for things over the course of years and some of them drifted out of your active memory.

Don't do anything with what you find yet. Don't try to close accounts or organize anything. Just let yourself see how many surface. That's your baseline. Keep that inbox window open or jot down a few notes, because you'll refer back to it during the week.

The second part is a braindump. Open a notebook or a blank document and spend ten minutes writing down every account you can think of without looking anything up. Just what comes to mind, in whatever order it surfaces. Email addresses, bank accounts, streaming services, social media, whatever floats up. Don't stop to research. Don't worry about what you're missing. You're not trying to finish the list. You're priming the pump.

Now, a word about those forgotten accounts you surfaced in the search. You don't need to do anything dramatic with them right now. For most of them, the right answer is simply to add them to your inventory list during the relevant category day. If you find an account you genuinely no longer want or need, closing it is a reasonable choice, but it's not urgent and it's not required to complete the inventory. Just note that it exists.

It's worth knowing that dormant accounts aren't entirely harmless. An old account sitting forgotten at a service you haven't used in years is still a potential entry point for someone who isn't you, particularly if it uses an old password you've reused elsewhere. You don't need to spend this week closing every forgotten account you find. But flagging the ones that surprise you, especially old email addresses or financial accounts you'd forgotten about, is a sensible precaution you can act on later.

When both parts are done, you're done for day zero. Close the laptop. The actual week starts tomorrow.

Seven Days, One Category Each Day

Here's where most people go wrong. They try to build the whole list in one sitting, run out of steam halfway through, and never finish.

Don't do that.

Instead, give yourself seven days and cover one category per day. One category. You can spend as little as fifteen minutes on it. When you've covered that category, you're done for the day. Close the notebook. Put down the pen. You've done what you needed to do.

The next category will be there tomorrow.

Here are the seven categories. I want to spend a moment on each one so you know exactly what you're looking for when your day arrives.

Day One: Email Accounts

Start here because email is the thread that connects almost everything else. Almost every account you've ever created online was tied to an email address at signup. That makes your email accounts uniquely important on this list.

Most people have more than one. There's the main address they check every day. There's often an old one from a previous internet provider or cable company. Many people have a Gmail they set up because someone told them to. Some people have a separate address created specifically for signing up for things they didn't want cluttering their main inbox.

Write them all down. Even the ones you rarely check. Even the ones you're not sure are still active. If a family member ever needs to reset a password on one of your other accounts, they'll need access to whichever email address that account was registered under. An email address you've forgotten about can become a wall they can't get past.

When you've listed your email accounts, you're done for

the day.

Day Two: Financial Accounts

This category is broader than most people expect. Yes, it includes your bank. But it also includes investment accounts, retirement accounts, and credit card management websites. It includes PayPal, Venmo, and Zelle if you use them. It includes any site where you've stored a credit card number, and any place where a recurring charge is being processed each month.

When you list each financial account, note whether any recurring charges draw from it. Your family will need that information quickly—Chapter Six covers why it matters and exactly what to do about it.

One more category belongs here that most people forget entirely: loyalty programs. Airline miles, hotel points, and credit card rewards accounts all have real financial value, and they are among the most commonly overlooked digital assets in an estate. A substantial balance of airline miles can be worth hundreds of dollars, sometimes more, and most programs have a process for transferring points to a surviving family member, but only if the family knows the account exists. Add your frequent flyer accounts, hotel rewards memberships, and any credit card points programs to your financial list today. The login is usually a separate account from the credit card itself, so note where those credentials live.

When you've listed your financial accounts, you're done for the day.

Day Three: Devices

This one surprises people because devices don't feel like

accounts. But they belong on the list for a specific reason.

Your smartphone, tablet, and computer are the containers that hold almost everything else. A locked phone without a known PIN can be permanently inaccessible, even to people with legitimate legal authority over your estate. Security researchers and estate planning attorneys both flag this as one of the most common and entirely avoidable problems families face. There is often no back door. A locked device is a wall, and there is frequently no door in.

A woman named Patrice learned this the hard way after her mother passed away. Her mother had been a prolific correspondent, the kind of person who wrote long, thoughtful messages to friends and family and kept every reply. Patrice knew those messages existed. She had received hundreds of them herself over the years. What she didn't know was the six-digit PIN on her mother's iPhone, and neither did anyone else in the family. Her mother had changed it at some point and never mentioned the new one to anybody.

Patrice contacted Apple. Apple explained, politely and correctly, that they could not bypass the device's encryption under any circumstances. That is not a policy decision. It is a technical reality. The data on a locked iPhone is encrypted in a way that Apple itself cannot access.

What Patrice would have found, had she known that PIN, was a record of her mother's inner life in the last years of hers. Thousands of messages with old friends from decades past, people Patrice had heard mentioned but never met. A notes app filled with observations, family stories her mother had been meaning to write down properly, a running list of things she was grateful for. Photographs taken on walks, of birds at a feeder outside her window, of her grandchildren asleep on the couch. A voice memo, recorded on a Sunday afternoon, of her mother singing a song she had learned as a girl.

None of it was gone in any dramatic sense. It was all still there, sitting on the phone, perfectly preserved. It was simply unreachable. And eventually the phone's battery died, and the phone was set aside, and the life it contained stayed locked inside it.

For each device, note what it is, what it's primarily used for, and whether it's protected by a PIN or passcode. Then, separately from this list, write those PINs down somewhere your trusted person can find them. Not on a sticky note on the device. Somewhere secure but accessible to the right person.

While you're thinking about devices, include any smart home technology you use. If you have a Ring doorbell or security camera system, a smart thermostat like a Nest, a smart door lock, or a home hub like Amazon Echo or Google Home, those are all tied to accounts that your family or executor will need access to. If something happens to you and someone needs to check on the house, secure it, or prepare it for sale, they'll need to know these systems exist and how to reach them. You don't need to explain how any of it works. You just need to leave a note that says something like "Ring security cameras, account under this email, login in the notebook." That breadcrumb is enough. The goal isn't for your family to become smart home experts overnight. It's simply to make sure they're not locked out of systems that are actively running in your home.

When you've listed your devices and noted their PINs, you're done for the day.

If you use a Samsung phone, note it on your list—Samsung runs its own cloud backup service separate from Google, and Chapter Four walks through how to check both.

Day Four: Subscriptions

Streaming services are the obvious ones. But this category also includes news sites, software subscriptions, cloud storage services, apps with monthly or annual fees, and any membership site that sends you a renewal notice.

The inbox search from day zero will help here. Go back and look at what surfaced. Pull out anything with a recurring charge. If you see a monthly receipt or a renewal notice from a service, that service belongs on your list.

Two things matter for each subscription: knowing it exists, and knowing which payment method it's attached to. Both pieces of information help your family stop charges quickly after you're gone.

Dennis's daughter Janet discovered just how much this matters about three months after her father died. She had done a reasonable job closing his major accounts and notifying the right institutions. What she hadn't done was go looking for subscriptions, because she didn't know to look. The charges that kept appearing on her father's credit card statement were small enough that they didn't immediately alarm anyone. Eight dollars here. Twelve dollars there. A fifteen-dollar renewal for a piece of software Dennis had used once and forgotten about.

By the time Janet noticed the pattern and started tracking them down, the card had been charged nearly two hundred dollars for services nobody was using and nobody wanted. Cancelling each one required its own phone call or online process, and several of them required access to Dennis's email to complete the cancellation. It took her the better part of a weekend to sort out what a single page of notes would have resolved in an afternoon.

But the wasted money wasn't what stayed with Janet. It was

what she learned about her father in the process of tracking the subscriptions down.

There was a monthly charge for an online course platform. Dennis had been taking classes. Spanish, it turned out, at 74 years old, working through beginner lessons on Tuesday and Thursday evenings when the house was quiet. There was a subscription to a genealogy service Janet hadn't known about, and when she finally got into the account she found eighteen months of careful research into a branch of the family that had emigrated from Poland three generations back, names and dates and scanned documents Dennis had never mentioned to anyone. There was a small recurring donation to a charity that worked with homeless veterans, set up years earlier and quietly renewed every year.

Janet had thought she knew her father well. She did know him well. But a list of his subscriptions turned out to be a map of his private enthusiasms, the things he cared about and worked on in the hours when nobody was watching. She wishes she had known while he was alive to ask him about them.

A simple list would have given her that chance.

When you've listed your subscriptions, you're done for the day.

Day Five: Photos

Photos deserve their own day because for most people they represent the most emotionally significant part of their digital life. Not the most financially significant. The most personally significant. The pictures of people who are no longer here. The record of your family growing up. The images that exist nowhere else.

The question for day five is simple: where do your photos actually live?

They might be on your phone. They might be backed up automatically to iCloud if you have an iPhone, or to Google Photos if you have an Android. They might be in Amazon Photos, which comes free with a Prime membership and which many people have activated without quite realizing it. They might be on a Windows PC in the Pictures folder, or copied onto an external hard drive sitting on a shelf somewhere.

Thomas almost lost everything. He had spent fifteen years photographing his family on a series of Android phones, each one backing up automatically to Google Photos without him thinking much about it. When he upgraded to an iPhone, a well-meaning family member helped him set up iCloud and, in the process, turned off the Google Photos backup without realizing what it was. For eight months, Thomas's new photos went to iCloud while his old ones sat in Google Photos, unsynced and slowly drifting toward the storage limit that would eventually stop the service from retaining them.

He found out by accident, when his grandson asked to see a photo from a family trip several years earlier and Thomas went looking for it. It took him two hours, one phone call to a tech-savvy nephew, and a considerable amount of anxiety to sort out where everything was and confirm that nothing had actually been lost. He got lucky. But the experience rattled him enough that he sat down that same week and wrote out exactly where every photo he owned actually lived.

Most people's photos live in more than one place, and not all of those places are obvious. Write down every location you can think of where a photo of yours might exist. For each one, note whether it's a service that requires a login, and if so, roughly where that login information is stored.

Flag these entries in your list. Write "photos here" next

to each one so that whoever manages your estate knows what they're dealing with before they make any decisions. Decades of family photographs deserve more than an accidental deletion.

When you've accounted for your photos, you're done for the day.

One thing worth knowing before you start: most people's photos live in more places than they expect, and backup is frequently stalled without the owner realizing it. Chapter Four covers the full picture—where photos actually live, how to check whether your backup is working, and what to do if it isn't. If photos are your main concern, you may want to read that chapter alongside this one.

Day Six: File Storage

File storage is the category that varies most from person to person. Some people have very little. Others have years of documents, spreadsheets, writing, and records scattered across multiple services and devices.

Start with the most common places files tend to live.

If you have a Windows computer, the Documents folder is the first place to check. This is where Windows automatically saves files from Word, Excel, and most other programs, and it tends to accumulate years of material that people forget is there. Tax returns, letters, financial records, personal writing. If you haven't looked in your Documents folder recently, it's worth a few minutes to see what's there.

If you use a Mac, the equivalent is the Documents folder in Finder, along with the Desktop, which many people use as an informal filing system.

Beyond the computer itself, file storage increasingly lives in the cloud. Dropbox, Google Drive, OneDrive, and iCloud

Drive are the most common services. Some people use one. Some use several, having signed up for different ones at different times for different reasons. Your inbox search from day zero may have surfaced some of these.

When a man named Arthur died at 79, his daughter Meg was the one who sat down at his old Windows laptop to see what was there. She wasn't expecting much. Arthur had been a quiet, private man, not someone she associated with spending time on a computer. She opened the Documents folder mostly out of obligation.

What she found was a folder labeled "Family" containing nearly four hundred pages of writing. Memories of his childhood. Stories about his parents, both long gone. A detailed account of how he had met Meg's mother. Letters he had written but never sent. Notes on things he wanted his grandchildren to know about the family history. Arthur had been writing for years and had never mentioned it to anyone.

Meg sat at the laptop for three hours that afternoon, reading. She has since printed everything and had it bound for each of her children.

None of it would have been found if she hadn't known to look in the Documents folder. Arthur hadn't hidden it. He simply hadn't thought to tell anyone it was there.

For each storage location, note what it is, roughly what it contains, and whether it requires a login. You don't need to catalog every file. You just need to make sure your family knows these places exist and how to find them.

When you've accounted for your file storage, you're done for the day.

Day Seven: Social Media and Online Communities

Facebook and Instagram are the obvious entries here. But this category also includes accounts that hold real personal history and are easy to overlook.

The genealogy site you joined a few years ago. The neighborhood forum. The hobby community you've been part of for a decade. A church or club website where you have a login. These accounts often hold years of conversation, photographs, and personal records that your family might want access to, or at least want to know about.

You don't have to make any decisions right now about what should happen to these accounts after you're gone. That conversation comes in a later chapter. For now, just write them down.

When you've listed your social media and online communities, you're done. Not just for the day. The inventory is built.

If you make it through even three or four of these categories, you have done something most people never do. You have a partial map, and a partial map is infinitely more useful to your family than none at all. Keep going when you can. Don't feel like you're being pressured. What you have already written down is already working.

What Format Should You Actually Use

People ask about this constantly, and the honest answer is that almost any format works as long as you'll actually use it.

A spiral notebook is fine. A Word document is fine. A sheet of paper in a filing folder is fine. The SANS Institute, one of the leading cybersecurity research organizations in the country, explicitly recommends that keeping a secure notebook in a locked file cabinet is a perfectly sound approach.

Not a compromise. A recommended practice.

If you want to use a spreadsheet, use one. But don't let the question of format become the reason you don't start. I've seen people spend months researching the perfect app before writing a single account down. A legal pad and a pen will do everything a $50 app will do for this particular task.

What matters more than format is redundancy. Keep at least two copies. If you have a digital document, print it out. If you have a paper list, take a photo of it and store the photo somewhere your family can find it. A physical folder in a filing cabinet, labeled something obvious like "Digital Info" or "For My Family," is exactly as effective as it sounds. Estate planning attorneys consistently recommend the combination of a physical copy and a digital backup, not because either is unsafe alone, but because having both means one survives whatever happens to the other.

Keeping It Current Without Making It a Project

Here is the mistake almost everyone makes after finishing the inventory: they build the list once, feel relieved, and never touch it again.

Two years later the list is partially wrong. Accounts they closed are still on it. New accounts they opened aren't. Estate planning guides note, with some bluntness, that a digital inventory two years out of date may be only marginally better than no inventory at all, because it sends your family searching for things that no longer exist while missing things that do.

The fix is not a big annual review, though an annual review is not a bad idea. The fix is a small habit. When a billing email lands in your inbox for something not on your list, add it. When you close an account, cross it off. When you set up a new service, add it the same day.

Ten seconds in the moment. An hour of frustrating archaeology if you let it accumulate.

The triggers worth paying attention to are the routine ones you already encounter. A renewal notice arrives for a news subscription you forgot about. That's a trigger. You get a new phone and spend an afternoon setting it up. That's a trigger. You cancel a streaming service you haven't used in months. That's a trigger. You open a new credit card with a better rewards program. That's a trigger. None of these moments requires more than a minute of attention to your list. The renewal notice either confirms something already on the list or tells you something new belongs there. The new phone is a new device entry. The cancelled service gets crossed off. The new card gets noted next to whichever subscriptions you move onto it.

You are not maintaining a database. You are keeping a living document the same way you'd keep a running grocery list. You add things when you think of them. You cross things off when they're done. The list is never perfect and it doesn't need to be. It just needs to be current enough that the person who eventually relies on it isn't chasing ghosts.

Treat the list the way you'd treat an address book. Not something you rebuild from scratch every year. Something you keep current because keeping it current is easier than not.

What Good Enough Actually Looks Like

I want to push back against the idea that this has to be comprehensive to count.

A man named Harlan, a retired high school principal, decided to build his inventory after his wife mentioned it at dinner. He was not particularly organized. He described himself, without embarrassment, as someone who piled things rather than filed them. He sat down on a Saturday morning with a yellow legal pad and wrote down everything he could think of. Forty minutes. Twenty-eight accounts. He knew he'd missed some. He put the list in a folder in his desk drawer, told his wife where it was, and considered himself done.

When Harlan had a stroke eight months later, his wife and daughter were able to reconstruct his digital life in a few days rather than a few weeks. The list wasn't perfect. Four accounts on it had been closed. Three accounts he'd opened weren't on it. But it gave them a starting point that made everything else manageable.

That is what good enough looks like. Not perfect. Not exhaustive. Just enough of a map that the people you love aren't standing in the dark.

Harlan's legal pad had cross-outs and question marks and a note in the margin that said "check on this." It was also the thing that kept his family from drowning.

I mention this because I know how the perfectionist instinct works on a project like this. You start the list and immediately notice the gaps. You can't remember the exact name of that one streaming service. You're not sure whether you still have that old Hotmail address or whether it expired years ago. You don't know if the investment account your brother helped you set up counts as an account you manage or one he manages. And so you stop, intending to figure those things out first, and the list sits unfinished.

Don't let that happen. A list with gaps is not a failed list. It's an incomplete list, and incomplete lists can be finished. A list that never gets started cannot.

Write down what you know. Leave a question mark next to what you're unsure about. Come back to the gaps later, or don't. The twenty-eight accounts Harlan wrote down in forty minutes were not the whole picture. They were enough of the picture. That's the standard you're aiming for.

A Note on Shared Households

If you share your life with a spouse or partner, the inventory works best as a household project rather than two individual ones.

This doesn't mean sitting down together simultaneously. It means that shared accounts, jointly held financial relationships, and streaming services in one person's name that both people use all belong on a single household list rather than two separate lists that each capture half the picture.

It also tends to surface something worth knowing. In most households, one person handles the financial accounts and the other handles the utility payments and subscriptions. Neither has a complete picture of the whole. The inventory makes that division of digital labor visible, often for the first time.

That conversation is worth having while you can still have it together.

Consider what happens when it doesn't happen. A woman named Ruth took over her household finances after her husband Gene passed away. She was capable and organized, and she expected the transition to be hard but manageable. What she hadn't anticipated was the number of small online accounts Gene had handled quietly for years. The electric bill, paid through a utility website she'd never logged into. The homeowner's insurance, renewed annually through a portal she didn't know existed. The family's antivirus software, set to autorenew on a credit card she'd already cancelled.

None of these were complicated. None of them were hidden. Gene simply handled them, the way Ruth handled other things, and neither of them had ever thought to make a list that covered both halves of the household.

Ruth sorted it out. It took longer than it needed to, and it added stress to an already difficult time. A shared inventory, even a rough one, would have changed that.

If you and your partner decide to build this together, the simplest approach is to work through the same seven categories but compare notes at the end of each day. You'll quickly discover which accounts you both knew about, which ones only one of you knew about, and which ones neither of you can quite account for. That last category, the ones neither of you can account for, is often the most interesting and occasionally the most important.

What To Do This Week

The plan below runs eight days in total. Day zero happens before the week starts, whenever you have twenty quiet minutes. The seven category days can start any day you like. Each task is self-contained. When you finish a day's task, you're finished for that day. No carrying over. No catching up. No pressure to keep going.

Day zero is the preparation step. Do the inbox search using the phrases described earlier in this chapter. Then spend ten minutes on the braindump, writing down whatever accounts come to mind without looking anything up. When both are done, close the laptop. You've set yourself up for a smooth week.

Day one is email accounts. Day two is financial accounts.

Day three is devices and their PINs. Day four is subscriptions. Day five is photos. Day six is file storage. Day seven is social media and online communities.

Each day, when the category is done, you're done. The list will still be there tomorrow. The only thing left to do after day seven is decide where the completed inventory will live and tell one trusted person where to find it. Your spouse, your adult child, your executor, whoever makes sense. You don't need to share what's on it. Just make sure someone knows where it is.

That's the whole job. Eight days of short, focused tasks. And what you'll have at the end is something most people never get around to building.

CHAPTER THREE

PASSWORDS, ACCESS, AND WHO GETS IN WHEN YOU CAN'T

How to make sure the right people can reach your digital life and the wrong ones can't

Walter had been the one who handled everything. That was just how his marriage worked, and neither he nor his wife Diane pretended otherwise. Walter paid the bills online, managed their investments, kept track of the insurance renewals, and maintained a tidy little system on his laptop that held most of the passwords he used. It wasn't a real system, exactly. More of a document he'd started years ago and kept adding to. He knew where it was. Diane didn't.

When Walter had a stroke at seventy-one, he survived. That part was a relief that brought Diane to her knees in the hospital parking lot. But he was in rehabilitation for six weeks, and the digital life he'd built kept running without anyone at the controls. As Chapter Two covers, the autopay problem alone can create weeks of chaos when the person who set everything up is suddenly unreachable. What made Walter's situation specifically a password problem was this: Diane couldn't get into a single account to see what was running, what was due, or what needed her attention. The accounts existed. The money was there. She just couldn't get in.

Diane's situation is not unusual. In fact, a version of it plays out in families every single day. The person who managed the accounts gets sick, gets hurt, or dies. And the people left to sort it out discover that love and trust turn out to be no substitute for a password.

This chapter is about fixing that. Not in a complicated way. In the way a reasonably capable person can actually accomplish in a few evenings.

If you built your account inventory in Chapter Two, even an incomplete one, you have already done the hardest part of digital estate planning. Everything in this chapter builds on that foundation. Knowing where your accounts are is only half of what your family needs. The other half is making sure they can actually get in when the time comes78 and that covers everything from passwords and platform settings to photos, finances, social media, and the conversation you need to have with the people you trust. That is what the rest of this book is for.

You are not starting over. You are going deeper.

The Problem Isn't Forgetting—It's the System

Most people already know they should have some kind of plan for their passwords and accounts. The problem isn't awareness. The problem is that most of the solutions people actually use are either insecure, incomplete, or both.

Here is what the most common approaches look like in practice. A piece of paper near the computer with a few passwords written on it. A note in the iPhone with login information. An email to an adult child that says "just in case." A mental note that "the kids know where to look." These approaches feel like planning. They are not.

Paper gets lost, found by the wrong person, or thrown away by a well-meaning relative who didn't know what it was. A note in your phone is inaccessible if the phone is locked, which it almost certainly will be. An email sits in an inbox forever and becomes a security risk the moment anyone gains unauthorized access to that account. And the kids almost never actually know where to look.

Studies of how people actually manage passwords consistently turn up the same patterns: a significant share of people still rely on handwritten notes for at least some of their credentials, and many reuse the same passwords across a dozen or more accounts. Both habits create the same problem: when something goes wrong, the people who need access either can't find it or can find too much of it in the wrong places.

There is a better approach, and it doesn't require any special technical knowledge. It requires a little setup time and a decision about who you trust.

The Right Foundation: A Password Manager

A password manager is a secure application that stores all your usernames, passwords, and login information in one encrypted location. You create a single master password to open it. The app handles everything inside. Think of it as a very secure filing cabinet where all your digital keys live, protected by one combination you control.

The case for using one has nothing to do with being organized for its own sake. It has to do with what happens to your family if you don't. Without one, the people who need to access your accounts after you're incapacitated or gone face a scavenger hunt with no map. With one, they have a single place to go.

Password managers also solve a problem you may not have thought about yet: they work across everything. Your bank. Your email. Your Amazon account. Your Medicare portal. Your insurance login. Everything in one place, protected by one password you actually remember. That alone is worth the setup time.

Beyond storing passwords, several of the most widely used password managers now include something called emergency access. This feature was built specifically for the situation Walter and Diane found themselves in. It exists because the companies building these tools figured out that "what happens when something happens to you" is exactly the question their users were losing sleep over.

Here is how emergency access works in practice. You designate a trusted person inside the app. That person makes a request for access when they need it, which might be because you're in the hospital, incapacitated, or have died. You set a waiting period beforehand, typically somewhere between one and seven days. During that window, if you're actually fine and the request was premature, you can deny it with a tap. If the waiting period passes without a response from you, access is granted automatically.

That design is not an accident. It protects you from having your accounts handed over to someone who simply claims you're unavailable. And it protects your family from being locked out at the worst possible moment.

Which Password Manager to Use

There are several good options, and the honest answer is that any reputable one is better than none. Here are four that come up most often in serious recommendations.

Bitwarden is the one most frequently recommended for

people who want strong security without a complicated setup. It uses end-to-end encryption, meaning the company itself cannot read your passwords. The emergency access feature lets you designate up to five trusted contacts with different access levels: one option allows a contact to view your passwords, another allows them to manage your account on your behalf. The New York Times and Wired have both recommended it. Emergency access requires a paid subscription, which runs a few dollars a month. The free version is excellent for daily use, but the estate planning feature is in the premium tier.

1Password is another well-regarded option and is particularly worth considering if you want to share access with a spouse or partner while you're both alive. Its family plan is designed with shared household use in mind, which makes the ongoing management feel more natural for two people. It also includes an emergency kit, a printed document you create during setup that your family can use to access your account if needed.

Dashlane has a reputation for a cleaner, more approachable interface than some competitors. For people who find the setup of other password managers slightly intimidating, Dashlane tends to hold your hand a bit more during the onboarding process. It covers the basics well and is a legitimate choice if ease of use is your primary concern.

One thing worth knowing about Dashlane: its emergency access works differently from the others on this list. There is no trusted-contact designation or timed waiting period. Instead, you set it up yourself in advance by exporting an encrypted backup file of your entire vault, called a DASH file, and storing it somewhere your trusted person can find it later. You create a separate password just for that file and share that password with your contact separately.

When they need it, they download the file, create or use an existing Dashlane account, and import it. They then have access to everything that was in your vault at the time you exported it.

That last part is the catch. The DASH file is a snapshot, not a live connection. Every time you add a new account or change a password, you need to export a fresh file and make sure your trusted contact has the updated version. It works, but it requires ongoing maintenance in a way the other options do not. Dashlane's free plan was discontinued in September 2025, so a paid subscription is now required.

Proton Pass comes from the company behind Proton Mail, which has built a strong reputation for privacy-focused technology. Their emergency access feature, launched in August 2025, works much like Bitwarden's. You designate up to five trusted contacts inside your Proton account settings. When one of them needs access, they initiate a request from their own Proton account. You set a waiting period in advance, and if you don't respond before it expires, access is granted automatically. If you're fine and the request was premature, you can deny it with a tap at any point during that window.

What makes Proton's version stand out is the scope of access. A designated contact does not just get your passwords. They can also reach your Proton Mail, Proton Drive, and Proton VPN account data. If you use Proton's ecosystem already, a single emergency access setup covers your encrypted email, stored files, and all your passwords at once. Your contact needs a Proton account to initiate a request, but the free tier is sufficient on their end. Emergency access requires a paid Proton subscription on your end.

The differences between these four are real but not enormous. Pick one and set it up. The best password manager is the one you will actually use.

Before you set up any of the tools in this chapter, make sure you know which environments actually hold your data. You built that picture in Chapter Two. If you skipped ahead, go back and do Day Three and Day Five before continuing here. Knowing where your photos, email, and files actually live is what determines which of the access tools below you actually need.

Apple's Legacy Contact: Access to Your Entire Apple World

Apple's Legacy Contact feature is built directly into iPhone, iPad, and Mac settings, and it lets you designate someone who can access your entire iCloud account after you die. That means your photos, contacts, messages, notes, and files stored in iCloud Drive. You designate a trusted person, Apple generates an access key you share with them, and when the time comes they present that key along with a death certificate to complete the process. The access lasts three years, giving your family time to retrieve what matters. To set it up on an iPhone, go to Settings, tap your name at the top, select Sign-In and Security, and look for Legacy Contact. The process takes about fifteen minutes and is free.

Google's Inactive Account Manager: Access to Your Entire Google World

Google's Inactive Account Manager lets you designate up to ten trusted contacts and specify exactly which Google services each can access, whether that's Gmail, Google Photos, Google Drive, or a combination. You set an inactivity period between three and eighteen months, after which

Google notifies your contacts and grants them access to what you've specified. For anyone with years of family photos in Google Photos or a lifetime of email in Gmail, this is not a small thing. To set it up, go to myaccount.google.com and search for Inactive Account Manager. The setup takes about twenty minutes and costs nothing. Note that this is separate from Google's Recovery Contacts feature, which helps you get back into your own account. For estate planning, Inactive Account Manager is the one you want.

Choosing the Right Person—and Having the Conversation

The technology is the easier half of this. The harder half is deciding who gets access to what, and then actually telling them.

Most people's first instinct is to name the most technically capable person they know. That's not necessarily wrong, but technical skill is not the primary qualification. The right person is someone you trust completely, someone who will act in your interest and in the interest of your other loved ones without using access for their own benefit. Technical savvy can be learned. Trustworthiness cannot be installed.

It's also worth thinking about whether one person should hold all of it. There is nothing wrong with designating your adult daughter as your Apple Legacy Contact, your son as the emergency contact in your password manager, and a trusted friend as a backup for your Google account. You are not required to centralize everything. In some families, distributing access actually reduces friction rather than creating it.

Whatever you decide, the people you designate need to know. Don't surprise them. Having this conversation is not as difficult as most people fear. It's usually something along the lines of: "I've set things up so you can get into my accounts if something happens to me. Here's what that means and here's what I've done." Most adult children will feel relieved, not burdened. They have probably worried about exactly this.

One thing worth saying plainly: designating an emergency contact in a password manager or setting up a Legacy Contact does not replace a will, a power of attorney, or any other legal document. These tools give trusted people practical access to digital accounts. They don't confer legal authority over assets. If you don't have the legal documents in order, the digital access tools are still worth setting up, but they work alongside your estate planning, not in place of it.

The Specific Risk of Email and Text

Even after reading all of the above, some people will think: this is more complicated than I need. I'll just text my daughter the passwords.

Here is why that is a genuinely bad idea, and not just a theoretical one.

When you send a password in a text or an email, that password now lives in at least three places: your outbox, your recipient's inbox, and your cellular carrier's or email provider's servers. If any of those accounts is ever compromised, which happens more often than most people realize, every password you've shared that way is now visible to whoever got in. And because people tend to reuse passwords or use similar patterns, one exposed password often becomes a key that opens several doors.

There's also the more mundane problem: a text from three years ago that says "just in case, my email password is" is easy to forget about and hard to find when actually needed.

And if you've changed the password since then, which you should, the old one is sitting in a thread going nowhere.

The tools described in this chapter exist specifically because email and text are not the right way to share access credentials. Use them instead.

The Two-Factor Authentication Complication

There is one thing that can derail even the best-prepared family member, and it's worth mentioning directly. Many accounts now use two-factor authentication, which means logging in requires not just a password but also a code sent to a phone or generated by an app. If something happens to you, your trusted contact may have the password but not the device that receives the verification code.

This is a real problem, and it doesn't have a perfect solution. But there are a few things that help.

First, if you use a phone to receive verification codes, make sure your trusted contact knows that. More importantly, make sure they know how to contact your cell phone carrier to manage the account, since carriers can transfer number access in estate situations, though the process varies.

Second, some accounts allow backup codes, which are one-time codes generated when you set up two-factor authentication. If you have these, store them somewhere your trusted contact can find. Your password manager is a reasonable place.

A separate and increasingly common version of this problem involves authenticator apps. Google Authenticator, Microsoft Authenticator, and similar tools generate six-digit login codes directly on your phone rather than sending them by text. The code is produced by the app itself, which means no phone signal is required. But it also means that if your phone is locked, dead, or simply unavailable to a family member, those codes cannot be generated at all, even if the person has your correct password. Most services that support authenticator apps will automatically offer backup codes during the two-factor setup process. Those codes are one-time-use and they bypass the authenticator when the device isn't available. When you set up any account with an authenticator app, generate those backup codes and store them in your password manager. That single habit closes what is otherwise a hard-to-notice gap in your access plan.

Third, for the accounts that matter most, consider whether you can add a trusted person as a secondary phone number for two-factor verification while you're still here to do it. This isn't appropriate for every account, but for things like a primary email address or a financial account, it's worth considering. In a Google account, for example, you can do this at myaccount.google.com by going to Security, then clicking on 2-Step Verification, and looking for the Phone number option under the list of second steps. From there you can add a backup phone number that will also receive verification codes. It takes about two minutes and it means your trusted contact can get a login code sent directly to their phone when they need it.

Two-factor authentication exists to protect you, and it does that job well. The goal here is not to undermine it but to make sure your estate plan accounts for it.

The Phone Number Nobody Thinks to Keep

Here is something that happens in a lot of families, and it happens fast. A loved one dies on a Monday. By Wednesday or Thursday, someone calls the phone carrier to cancel the line because the bills will keep coming and it feels like one less thing to deal with. It is an entirely reasonable instinct.

It is also, depending on how the accounts were set up, a decision that can lock the family out of almost everything.

A phone number is not just a way to make calls. For most people, it is the hub of their entire verification system. Bank alerts go to that number. Login codes go there. The "verify it's you" prompts that appear when you try to sign in from a new device go there. Password reset links that require a confirmation code go there. The number is, in effect, a master key that sits underneath most of the other keys. Cancel it before you have accounted for all the accounts that depend on it, and those accounts become unreachable.

Picture how it plays out. A family member cancels the phone line on day three. On day five, they try to log into the primary email account. The email provider does not recognize the device, so it offers to send a verification code. That code goes to the canceled number. The number no longer exists. The email account cannot be reached. The email account is the recovery address for the bank. The bank is where the autopayments are running, including several that will overdraft or lapse in the next ten days. Each locked door leads to another locked door. None of this is malicious. It is just the shape of how these accounts are connected.

The practical guidance is this: before canceling any phone line, make a quick call to the carrier and ask about your options. Most carriers will let a family member keep the number active temporarily on a reduced plan, transfer it to an existing family account, or port it to a new line so it remains reachable. A single call before making any decisions will tell you which of those paths is available and what it costs. The phone bill can wait a few weeks. The accounts tied to that number cannot always wait to be sorted out.

You can prevent this problem entirely for your own family, and it requires very little. In your account inventory, note which accounts use your phone number for verification or password recovery. You do not need to list every account. Focus on the ones that matter most: your primary email, your bank, your investment accounts, your insurance portals. Then make sure the trusted person in your life knows not to cancel your phone line until those accounts have been checked, accessed, and handed off. A sentence in your digital inventory document is enough. "Do not cancel my phone number until you have access to these accounts." That sentence, in the right place, could save your family a week of frustration at the worst possible time.

The Shift to Passkeys

There is one more change happening in the background that is worth knowing about, because it affects the way families will access accounts in the years ahead. The technology industry is moving away from traditional passwords. The replacement is called a passkey, and it works differently from anything this chapter has described so far.

Instead of typing a password to log into your bank or your email, a passkey uses your device itself as the proof of identity. You hold up your phone, it recognizes your face or your fingerprint, and you're in. No password to remember. No password to type. The device does the work.

That sounds convenient, and it is. But it creates a specific estate planning problem that is easy to miss. If you set up a passkey for your bank, there is no traditional password for your password manager to save. The credential doesn't exist as a string of characters sitting in a vault somewhere. The credential is the device in your hand, unlocked by your face or your finger. Which means that if something happens to you and your trusted contact needs to get into that bank account, they don't need your password manager. They need your phone. And they need to be able to unlock it.

This is not a reason to avoid passkeys. They are genuinely more secure than passwords in most situations, and they will become the standard whether any of us opts in or not. But it does mean that the PIN or passcode you use to unlock your phone or computer belongs on the same list as your password manager's master password. Your trusted contact needs both.

Think of it this way. Your password manager is the key to your digital filing cabinet. Your device PIN is the key to a different filing cabinet that is growing larger every year. Right now those two cabinets hold different things. Over time, more and more of your accounts will live in the device cabinet rather than the password manager cabinet. Leaving both keys with someone you trust is the practical response to that shift.

If you're not sure whether any of your accounts use passkeys yet, check your bank's website or app settings. Many major banks and services began rolling out passkey support in 2024 and 2025. The option is usually listed under Security or Sign-In settings. If you've enabled it without quite realizing what it was, now you know what it means for the people who may one day need to reach those accounts on your behalf.

What Your Trusted Contact Actually Needs to Have

Meredith's mother had done everything right, by the usual standard. She'd set up emergency access in her password manager. She'd named Meredith as the designated contact. When her mother had a serious fall and spent several weeks in a rehabilitation facility, Meredith initiated the request through the app. She waited through the access period. Access was granted. And then she discovered she needed the master password to open the vault on her own device. The app on her mother's phone was already logged in, but Meredith was setting this up on her own device, and the master password was required to get started. Her mother was not always coherent at that point. Meredith had been designated. She had never been briefed.

The setup had been done. The handoff had never happened. Those two things are not the same.

So let's be specific about what a trusted contact actually needs. Not what tools you've set up. What they need to have, or know where to find, when the moment arrives.

They need the master password to your password manager, or they need to know exactly where it is written down. Not "somewhere safe." Somewhere specific. The desk drawer. The sealed envelope in the fireproof box. The exact location. If they cannot open the vault, the vault does not exist for them.

They need to know the PIN or passcode for your primary device. Without it, passkeys won't work and two-factor codes arriving by text cannot be read. This is not a minor detail. As more accounts move to passkey authentication, the device itself becomes the credential. If the screen is locked and no one knows the code, the device is a brick for estate planning purposes.

They need to know your primary email address. Not just the address itself, but the fact that this is the account where confirmation links and recovery messages will land. When they try to access your bank and a "verify your identity" email goes out, that email goes somewhere. They need to know where.

They need to know not to cancel your phone line in the first days, for the reasons covered just above. That instruction has to come from you, in advance, because the instinct to tidy up the bills is strong and completely understandable. A note in your inventory document is enough. The note just has to exist.

And if you use an authenticator app for any of your important accounts, they need to know whether backup codes exist and where they are stored. As noted earlier in this chapter, most services generate those codes at setup. If you saved them in your password manager, your trusted contact will find them there once they have the master password. If you printed them and put them in a folder somewhere, tell your contact that folder exists.

Designating someone is the first step. Telling them what they will need is the second step, and it matters just as much. A trusted contact who has been named but never briefed is a plan that exists on paper and nowhere else. They will do their best. Their best will run into walls.

The conversation you need to have does not have to be long. It does not require a lawyer or a spreadsheet or a formal meeting. It can be a single hour at the kitchen table, working through the list together. Here's where the password manager is. Here's the master password. Here's the phone passcode. Here's the email address. Here's why you should not cancel my phone right away. That hour, in full, is what separates a real plan from a good intention. Meredith's mother had a good intention. She just never had the hour.

If you have set up even one of the tools in this chapter, you have closed a gap that trips up families every single day. One legacy contact designation, one emergency access setup, one device PIN written down somewhere safe. Any one of those is a real thing your family will be grateful for. The rest can follow.

Back to Walter and Diane

Walter came home from rehabilitation eight weeks after his stroke. He was slower than before, needed a cane, and got tired in the afternoons. But he was home.

In the weeks he was gone, Diane had figured most of it out. She'd called the bank in person, explained the situation, produced the power of attorney their attorney had drawn up years before, and gotten access to the accounts she needed. She'd filed the insurance claim by phone after spending two hours on hold. She'd missed one autopayment and gotten a late fee she had to dispute. It was manageable. It was also exhausting and completely avoidable.

When Walter got home, he and Diane sat at the kitchen table with a laptop between them and spent an afternoon setting things up properly. They created a Bitwarden account. They went through Apple's Legacy Contact setup on both their phones. Walter walked Diane through the accounts that mattered, and they documented everything together. The document they made wasn't fancy. But it existed.

"I should have done this years ago," Walter said. Diane didn't disagree. But she also knew that most people don't do the things they should until something makes them do it. A stroke will do it. So will reading a chapter like this one. You get to choose which kind of motivation you prefer.

What To Do This Week

Start by choosing a password manager this week. You don't need to move all your passwords into it immediately. That can happen gradually over the coming weeks as you log into accounts normally. What matters this week is picking one and creating an account. Read through the options described in this chapter, Bitwarden, 1Password, Dashlane, Proton Pass, and choose the one that feels most suited to how you use your devices. If you're unsure, Bitwarden is a sensible starting point. Download it, set a strong master password, and store that master password somewhere physically safe. A sealed envelope with your other important documents is fine.

Once your password manager account exists, look into its emergency access feature. In Bitwarden, this is found under your account settings. Read through how it works, decide who you want to designate, and have that conversation with them before the week is out. Tell them what you're setting up and why. Ask if they're willing. It is almost certainly a shorter and easier conversation than you're imagining.

If you use an iPhone and haven't yet set up Apple's Legacy Contact, do it this week. Go to Settings, tap your name at the top, select Sign-In and Security, and look for Legacy Contact. It takes about fifteen minutes, it's free, and it's already on your phone.

If you use Gmail or Google Photos and haven't yet configured Google's Inactive Account Manager, go to myaccount.google.com before the week ends, search for Inactive Account Manager, and get it done. It takes about twenty minutes and costs nothing.

CHAPTER FOUR

DON'T LET YOUR LIFETIME OF PHOTOS DISAPPEAR

Your photos and videos are some of the most irreplaceable things you own—here's how to make sure your family can actually find and keep them.

Gloria was visiting her daughter for the weekend when her grandson, who is eight, asked to see a picture of his great-grandmother. Gloria knew exactly which photo she meant. It was one her mother had loved, taken at a family reunion in 1987, her mother laughing at something off-camera with her hair up the way she always wore it in summer.

Gloria knew she had it. She just couldn't find it.

She spent forty-five minutes going through her phone, then her tablet, then remembered she might have scanned it a few years ago and put it somewhere on her laptop. Her grandson lost interest after the first five minutes and went back to his video game. The photo turned up eventually, buried in a folder with an unhelpful name on a hard drive she'd almost forgotten she owned.

Later that night, lying awake, Gloria thought about what would happen to all of it when she was gone. Not the specific photo. All of it. The thousands of pictures she'd taken over the decades. The videos from her kids' school plays. The scanned slides her late husband had converted from his parents' collection in the 1990s. She had no idea, honestly, how much there was or where all of it lived. And she was absolutely certain her children had no idea either.

If you recognize yourself in any part of that story, this chapter is for you.

Why Digital Photos Are Harder to Protect Than Physical Ones

Physical photos are imperfect but forgiving. They sit in boxes, in albums, in shoeboxes under beds. Someone eventually finds the box. The worst that usually happens is that nobody knows who the people in the old pictures are, because no one thought to write names on the backs.

Digital photos are different. They are not sitting in a box. They are locked inside devices, hidden behind passwords, scattered across multiple services, sometimes backed up and sometimes not. When you are gone, nobody automatically gets access to any of it. The library doesn't open. The albums don't appear on the coffee table. Everything just sits there, unreachable, behind a screen that won't accept anyone else's fingerprint.

This is not a small problem. Most people over sixty have been taking digital photos for twenty years or more. A typical smartphone camera roll contains thousands of images. Add in photo services like iCloud or Google Photos, old hard drives, social media uploads, and whatever else accumulated over the years, and you may have a lifetime of visual history scattered across more locations than you can easily count.

What makes this different from almost every other kind of

loss is that the photos still exist. They are not gone. They are just locked away. And that specific kind of inaccessibility, knowing something is there but being unable to reach it, turns out to be its own particular grief for the families left behind.

Where Your Photos Actually Live

If you have already worked through Chapter Two's account inventory, you have a starting list of where your photos live. If you came straight to this chapter, that's fine. Everything you need is here. The short version: your photos are almost certainly in more places than you think. Your phone, iCloud or Google Photos, Facebook, Instagram, old hard drives, USB drives, CDs from the early 2000s, and possibly several cloud services you set up at different times for different reasons. The problem is not just access. It is that your family may not know which of those places exist, and neither tool covered in this chapter reaches all of them.

Apple Legacy Contact and Google Inactive Account Manager

If you use an iPhone, Apple's Legacy Contact feature gives a person you designate the ability to access your iCloud account after you die, which includes your entire iCloud Photos library. Every photo and video that has synced to iCloud is reachable through that process. Google's Inactive Account Manager covers the same ground for Google Photos, with one useful distinction: you can grant a trusted contact access to your photo library specifically while keeping other parts of your account, such as Gmail, separate. Google also has a policy of eventually deleting data from accounts that go inactive for two years, which means setting this up is not optional if Google Photos is where your pictures live. Chapter Three covers the setup for both features in full.

Amazon Photos and the Third Cloud You Forgot About

Before we leave the cloud services entirely, there is one more worth naming: Amazon Photos. If you have an Amazon Prime membership, you have unlimited photo storage through Amazon Photos included in it, and Amazon turns it on automatically for Prime members. A significant number of people have years of photos backed up there without knowing it, because they never set it up deliberately. It just happened.

Amazon does not have a Legacy Contact feature equivalent to Apple or Google. There is no built-in mechanism for a trusted person to access your Amazon Photos library after you die without your login credentials. That makes the shared folder approach described below especially important if Amazon Photos is where a significant portion of your pictures live. Get the important ones into a shared folder while you can, because there is no official back door for your family after the fact.

To check whether you have photos there, go to amazon.com, look for the Photos option in the main menu, and sign in. If photos appear, you have a library. Note it on your inventory from Chapter Two, and make sure the login is stored somewhere accessible in your password manager.

The 3-2-1 Rule You Have Probably Heard and Never Applied

People who work professionally in digital preservation talk about the 3-2-1 rule as the standard for protecting anything irreplaceable. Three copies of your data, stored on two different types of media, with one copy stored somewhere other than your home.

For most people, a practical version of this looks like: your photos exist on your phone, they are also backed up to a cloud service, and they have been copied to an external hard drive that lives somewhere other than your house (or that at least would survive a house fire, which an external drive in a fireproof safe could). You do not need to be obsessive about this. You need to not have a situation where every copy of your photos could disappear in a single event.

The honest conversation here is that a lot of people have zero redundancy. Their photos exist in one place, on one device, with no backup. If that device is lost, stolen, or fails, the photos are gone. That is the situation worth fixing first, before you worry about any of the estate planning questions.

A word on scope before we go further. Backing up your phone covers everything on it, not just photos. Your contacts, your texts, your apps, your settings. This chapter is focused on photos because they are the piece people feel most acutely when something goes wrong, but the habit of backing up applies to your whole device. Think of the photo backup as the reason to form the habit, not the only thing the habit is for.

Check whether your phone's camera roll is being backed up right now. On an iPhone, look in your settings under your Apple ID for the iCloud section, and find Photos. If iCloud Photos is toggled on, your camera roll is being backed up continuously whenever your phone is connected to WiFi. On an Android phone running Google Photos, open the app and look for a backup status indicator, usually visible on the main screen or under your account settings. If either of those settings is off, turn it on before you do anything else in this chapter.

Here is a wrinkle worth knowing about. Both iCloud and Google Photos give you a free storage allowance, but that allowance is modest, and if you have been taking photos for years it may already be full. When storage is full, new photos stop backing up, and the service does not always make this obvious. You may believe your photos are being backed up when they are not. The way to check on an iPhone is to go to Settings, tap your name, tap iCloud, and look at the storage bar at the top of the screen. If it is nearly full or shows a warning, your backup has likely stalled. On Google Photos, open the app and look for any notification about storage, or tap your profile picture and look for a storage indicator.

The fix is straightforward and inexpensive. Both Apple and Google offer paid storage upgrades for a few dollars a month, typically less than the cost of a single cup of coffee. The next tier up from the free allowance is usually enough to cover most people's entire photo library with room to spare. If your storage is full or close to it, upgrading is the right call. Losing years of photos because you did not want to spend a few dollars a month on storage is a trade most people would not make knowingly. The only reason it happens is that nobody checked.

Joanne had owned four iPhones over the years. Each time she got a new one, her carrier helped her transfer her contacts and apps, and she assumed the photos came along too. What nobody explained to her was that transferring a phone and backing up a phone are two different things. The photos moved from device to device, but they were never being copied anywhere outside the phone itself. When her most recent phone fell into a lake on a camping trip, she lost eight years of photos in an afternoon. Not locked away. Not inaccessible. Gone. She recovered a few hundred from Facebook and email threads, but the bulk of it, birthdays, holidays, ordinary days that had somehow mattered enough to photograph, was simply not there anymore. Joanne talks about it the way people talk about a small fire. Nothing irreplaceable in legal terms. Everything irreplaceable in the real ones.

The Photos That Live Outside the Cloud

The practical answer for those photos is to get them somewhere your family can access without waiting for you to die. That sounds blunt, but it is actually the simplest solution.

Cloud storage services like Google Drive and Dropbox let you create a shared folder, add your most important photos to it, and give family members direct access right now. They can browse the folder from their own devices, download what they love, and they do not need a death certificate or an access key to do it. The sharing happens in your lifetime, which is the whole point.

You do not have to share everything. A curated folder of your most meaningful photos, organized by decade or by family branch or however makes sense to you, is vastly more useful to your family than a chaotic archive they cannot navigate. Think about what you would want them to have, and put those things somewhere they can get to them.

Dropbox offers a Family plan with a dedicated shared folder designed specifically for this kind of use. Google Drive lets you share individual folders with anyone who has a Google account. Either approach works. The tool matters much less than the act of doing it.

The Prints in the Closet

This chapter is primarily about digital photos, but most people over sixty have a parallel problem sitting in a box somewhere: physical prints that have never been digitized. The school portraits. The vacation slides. The envelope of photographs from a grandparent's house that got handed down when nobody else wanted them. These are not digital assets, but they face their own version of the same risk. If nobody knows they exist, or nobody knows what they depict, they end up in an estate sale or a recycling bin.

Digitizing physical photos is a project worth doing, and it does not require any special equipment. Many public libraries offer scanning services. Retail chains that handle photo printing also offer digitizing services, where you drop off a box of prints and receive a USB drive or a download link. Mail-in services exist for larger collections or for slides and negatives, which require different equipment than a standard flatbed scanner. None of these options are expensive, and all of them convert something fragile and singular into something that can be copied, shared, and preserved.

You do not have to digitize everything. A box of five hundred prints from the 1970s is a large project. A box of the thirty or forty photos that actually matter, the ones you would rescue in a fire, is an afternoon. Start there. Get those specific photos into digital form, put them in the shared folder, and the rest can wait until you have more time or more motivation.

What Cannot Be Fixed After the Fact

The photos that break people's hearts after a loss are not always the ones they expected. Sometimes it is the opposite of what the caption problem describes. Not a photo with no context, but a photo with all the context, discovered too late for anyone to respond to it.

When Raymond died at seventy-nine, his daughter Elise was

clearing out his desk and found an old external hard drive in the back of the bottom drawer. The label on it, written in her father's careful block printing, said Genealogy Photos. She almost set it aside for the donation pile. She did not own the kind of cable that connected it to her laptop and had to order one online, which took three days to arrive.

What she found on it was years of work. Photographs organized by family branch, going back four generations. Scanned slides from the 1950s that Raymond had sent away to a conversion service years earlier. Individual folders for each of his grandchildren, each holding dozens of photos he had taken of them and captioned by hand. His own parents on their wedding day. His wife at twenty-two, standing in front of a car she had apparently been very proud of. Every single image had a note attached to it.

Elise has thought many times since about how close she came to donating that drive without ever plugging it in. Raymond had never mentioned it. There was no note in his papers pointing to it. She found it by luck, because she happened to open the right drawer on the right day. She has also thought about how many families find nothing at all, not because the person left nothing behind, but because what they left was on a device nobody thought to check.

The caption exercise at the end of this chapter is not just about labeling old faces. It is about making sure the things you have already done, the organizing, the collecting, the quiet work of preserving your family's record, do not stay invisible. Tell someone those folders exist. Put the most important ones in the shared folder now. Do not make your family discover them by accident after they have already grieved you.

The Tapes in the Closet

The physical print problem has a video equivalent that is, if anything, more urgent. Somewhere in a significant percentage of American homes over a certain age, there is a box of tapes. VHS tapes from the 1980s and 1990s. Hi8 cassettes from the camcorder era. MiniDV tapes from the early 2000s. Betamax, if you were an early adopter and slightly unlucky in the format wars. These tapes hold home video that exists nowhere else, and they are deteriorating. Magnetic tape degrades over time, and it degrades faster in storage conditions that are too warm, too cold, or too humid, which describes most garages and attics and basement closets.

The practical problem is that nobody owns a VHS player anymore. Or a Hi8 camera. The equipment to play those tapes has largely disappeared from ordinary households, which means even if your family knows the tapes exist and finds them after you are gone, they may have no way to watch them without a conversion service. And conversion services can only work with tapes that have not degraded past the point of playback.

Services exist that convert old home video tapes to digital files. You mail in the tapes, they convert them, and they send back a USB drive or an online download. The cost varies by volume and format. The urgency is real. A tape that works today may not work in five years. And unlike a digital file that fails silently, a degrading tape gives you no warning at all until you press play and find that the image has turned to noise.

If you have a box of old home video tapes, find it this week and open it. Look at the labels. If you can identify what is on them, write it on the box clearly in marker. If you cannot, note that the tapes exist and that they are unidentified, and put that note somewhere your family will find. Then look into a conversion service. This is one of the few items in digital estate planning where waiting genuinely makes things worse, because the raw material is physically decaying as you read this.

Voices From the Old Country

Vivian grew up hearing stories about her grandparents' village in rural Portugal. Her grandmother had come to the United States in the early 1950s, and she had brought almost nothing with her. No furniture, obviously. A few pieces of jewelry. And a small envelope of photographs.

When Vivian's grandmother died at ninety-one, those photographs went into a box that sat in Vivian's mother's closet for years. They were eventually scanned by a cousin who had gotten interested in genealogy, and the scans were emailed around to various family members, some of whom saved them and some of whom did not.

Vivian cannot tell you right now where those scans are. She thinks she has them on an old laptop. She is not certain. The physical originals are still in her mother's closet, and her mother is eighty-three and has not organized her own digital files in any meaningful way. There are photos on her mother's phone that nobody else has seen. There is a Facebook account with fifteen years of uploads in it. And there is a stack of printed photos from the 1990s that have never been digitized.

None of this is a crisis yet. It will become one, eventually, for whoever ends up trying to sort it out.

The genealogical research organizations that study this problem consistently reach the same conclusion: captioned, organized photographs are among the most valuable things you can leave behind. Not in a sentimental way, though they are that too. In a historical way. A photograph of your grandmother at twenty-five is information. A photograph of your grandmother at twenty-five, with a note explaining where and when it was taken and what was happening in her life at that moment, is a document that your great-grandchildren might treasure for reasons you cannot currently imagine.

The Caption Problem

There is a specific failure mode that repeats itself across families, which is that photos exist but no one knows who is in them. The person who knew is gone. The names are lost. The faces are just faces.

Genealogists call this the caption problem, and it is the single most common regret they hear from people who come to them wanting to research their family history. Not that the photos don't exist. That the photos exist but are unidentified.

The solution is almost embarrassingly simple, and it requires no technology at all. You write things down. Not an extensive biography. Two or three sentences. This is my mother's sister, Loretta, at the 1962 World's Fair in Seattle. She was twenty-four. She would go on to become a nurse and spend thirty years working in pediatric care. That is enough. That is, in fact, more than most people leave behind.

For digital photos, a text file in the same folder as the images works perfectly well. For shared folders, a document labeled something like Notes on the Photos is immediately useful to whoever finds it. If you use Apple Photos, tap the photo, swipe up from the bottom of the screen, and tap the caption field that appears below the image. In Google

Photos, open the photo, tap the three-dot menu in the upper right, select Edit Info, and type your description there. Both applications attach those captions to the image itself, so they travel with the photo when it is downloaded or shared.

You do not have to caption every photo you have ever taken. Start with the oldest, the rarest, and the ones where you are the only person still alive who knows who is in them. Those are the ones that will be lost when you go.

The Facebook and Instagram Problem

A significant portion of most people's photo history lives on social media, and social media operates by its own rules that are worth understanding before you assume your photos are safe there.

Facebook allows you to designate a Legacy Contact, which is a person who can manage your memorialized profile after you die. They can change the profile photo and cover photo, accept friend requests, and pin a post at the top of your profile. What they cannot do is log into your account, read your messages, or download your complete photo archive. That access requires you to take action before you die.

Facebook has a tool called Download Your Information that lets you export your complete data, including all photos and videos you have ever posted, in a single downloadable file. If you have fifteen years of photos on Facebook that exist nowhere else, downloading that archive and saving it somewhere your family can access it is worth doing. The option is in your Facebook settings under Your Facebook Information.

Instagram's approach is different. After a death, a family member can request that an account be memorialized, which preserves the profile and posts but prevents anyone from logging in. The photos stay visible but nobody can download them. The practical implication is the same: if Instagram posts represent a significant portion of your photo history, the time to download and save them is now, not later.

Neither platform makes this process particularly easy, which is itself an argument for not treating social media as your primary photo storage. The photos you post there should also exist somewhere else, somewhere that does not require a death certificate or a formal request process to retrieve them.

Once you have set up a shared folder and configured whatever access tools fit your situation, let your family know they exist. A brief note or a short conversation is enough: here is where the photos are, here is how to reach them, here is what I have set up so you will not be locked out. The fuller framework for how to have that conversation, and what else belongs in it, is in Chapter Seven.

A Note on Video

Everything in this chapter applies equally to video, and video has one additional complication worth noting. Video files are large. A single ten-minute home video can easily be a gigabyte. A collection of home videos from your children's childhood can be dozens or hundreds of gigabytes. That means the backup and sharing strategies that work for photos may need some adjustment for video.

Cloud services impose storage limits, and the free tier on both iCloud and Google Photos fills up faster than most people expect. If you have a significant video library, you may have already exceeded your free allowance, or you may be paying for additional storage without fully understanding what is and is not backed up.

Check your storage status. Both iCloud and Google Photos show your current usage somewhere in their settings, and both will tell you if you are running low. If you are close to your limit, either expand your storage plan or start making decisions about what gets backed up and what gets stored elsewhere.

Video is also where external hard drives earn their keep. A large-capacity external drive is inexpensive and can hold a genuinely enormous amount of video. Copying your home video collection to an external drive, labeling it clearly, and putting it somewhere your family knows about is one of the more lasting gifts you can give them.

What To Do This Week

The first thing to do this week is confirm your photos are actually being backed up, and that the backup has not stalled because storage is full. On an iPhone, check that iCloud Photos is turned on in your settings, then check the iCloud storage bar to make sure it is not full. On an Android phone running Google Photos, confirm that backup is active and look for any storage warning in the app. If storage is full on either service, the paid upgrade costs a few dollars a month and is worth it. A backup that stopped working six months ago because the storage filled up is the same as no backup at all.

The second thing is to create a shared folder in Google Drive or Dropbox and put your most important photos in it, then share access with the family members who should have it. This does not have to be everything. A curated folder of your two hundred most meaningful photos, organized in a way that makes sense, is more useful to your family than a chaotic archive of ten thousand images. They can access it now, from their own devices, with no death certificate required. Start small and add to it.

The third thing, and do not underestimate this one, is to find five photos where you are the only person who knows who is in them or what was happening, and write two or three sentences of context for each one. Put those notes somewhere they will be found with the photos. This is the kind of thing that cannot be done after you are gone, and the value of it only becomes apparent later, when someone is sitting with a photograph and wishing they could ask you about it.

None of these tasks requires technical expertise. They require thirty minutes to a few hours of your time, spread across a week. The families that do not have to grieve both the person and the inaccessible library of memories they left behind are the families whose loved ones did this work.

CHAPTER FIVE

WHAT HAPPENS TO YOUR SOCIAL MEDIA WHEN YOU DIE?

Your accounts will keep running long after you're gone—unless you tell them not to.

It was eleven months after her husband died when Noreen got the notification.

She was standing in her kitchen, phone in hand, reading a birthday reminder Facebook had sent her. It was for Martin. His birthday was in four days. Facebook was suggesting she wish him a happy birthday.

Martin had died of a heart attack the previous January. He was sixty-seven. Noreen had been the one to call their son, their daughter, Martin's sister in Phoenix. She had sat at a kitchen table surrounded by people for a week and then alone for the better part of a year. She knew, in every way a person can know something, that Martin was gone.

And here was Facebook, cheerful as ever, reminding her to write on his wall.

She put the phone face-down on the counter and didn't pick it up again until the next morning.

If you've lost someone in the past few years, you may have

had a version of this experience. Social media platforms have no way of knowing when a user dies unless someone tells them. Until someone does, the account keeps running on its own logic. Birthday reminders go out. Memory posts surface. "You haven't connected with Martin lately" suggestions appear in other people's feeds. On some platforms, the algorithm actively promotes old posts because engagement is the goal, and an old post with emotional resonance gets a lot of engagement.

None of this is malicious. The platforms are not trying to hurt anyone. They are simply running the programs they were designed to run, indifferent to the fact that one of their users is no longer here to see it.

The question this chapter is trying to answer is: what can you do now, while you are here, so that the people who love you don't have to stand in their kitchen feeling blindsided by a birthday reminder?

What Your Accounts Are Doing Right Now

Think about how many social platforms you're on. Facebook is the obvious one for most people in this age group. Instagram, possibly, if a family member talked you into it a few years ago. LinkedIn if you worked professionally and haven't gotten around to closing the account. Pinterest, perhaps. YouTube if you've watched enough videos that you ended up with an account attached.

Each of those accounts is active right now. Active in the sense that it exists, that it is accessible to the platform's systems, and that the platform is doing things with it. Suggesting you as a connection to other people. Including you in memory features. Continuing to accept friend requests in your name if someone sends them.

When someone dies and no one notifies the platforms, that activity continues indefinitely. Researchers who study digital afterlife have documented accounts remaining active and generating automated interactions for years, sometimes decades, after a person's death. The platform has no idea. Why would it?

There is also a security dimension that often gets overlooked. A social media account belonging to a deceased person is, from the perspective of a bad actor, an attractive target. The account owner is not checking it. Nobody is watching for unusual login attempts. The email address and phone number associated with the account may no longer be monitored. Criminals who specialize in account takeover know this. A hijacked account belonging to someone who is gone can be used to run scams targeting that person's friends and family, who may be slow to question a message that appears to come from someone they knew.

This is not a reason to panic. It is a reason to make a plan.

The Specific Problem of Memory Features

Most of the major social platforms now have features designed to surface old content. Facebook's "On This Day" and "Memories" features pull up posts from previous years and invite you to reshare them. Facebook also curates photo collages from old albums and posts them automatically. These are popular features that most living users enjoy.

When the account belongs to someone who has died, those same features become something entirely different for the people who were connected to that person. A memory post showing a video of someone who died six months ago, appearing in a family member's feed on a random Tuesday, is not a pleasant surprise. For many grieving people it is a genuine shock, and not always a welcome one.

Donna experienced this eighteen months after her mother passed. A video appeared in her Facebook feed, generated automatically by one of the platform's memory features. It was a short clip of Donna's mother at a family gathering three years earlier, laughing and saying something to someone off-camera. Her mother's account had never been memorialized. Nobody had contacted Facebook. The account was just sitting there, and Facebook's algorithm had found a video it thought Donna would enjoy.

Donna did not enjoy it. Not because the video wasn't precious to her, it was, but because she wasn't ready for it, hadn't chosen to see it, hadn't been asked. It arrived like a visitor who walks through the door without knocking.

"I wish I'd been the one to decide when to watch that," she said later. "I would have wanted to sit down and be ready. Instead I was just scrolling and suddenly there she was."

That is the experience your family will have if your accounts are left unattended. The choice about when and how to encounter you after you're gone gets made by an algorithm, not by the people who loved you.

What Memorialization Actually Does

Every major platform that has addressed this question has converged on a similar concept: memorialization. When an account is memorialized, it transitions from being an active user account to something more like a tribute space. The automated activity stops. Birthday reminders no longer go out. The account disappears from "People You May Know" suggestions. The algorithm stops treating it like a live user.

On Facebook, a memorialized account gets a "Remembering" label added to the name at the top of the profile. The posts and photos that were already there remain visible.

The account does not disappear. It simply stops behaving as though the person is still alive.

Facebook also allows you to designate a Legacy Contact, a person who can manage the memorialized profile after you die. Your Legacy Contact can pin a post at the top of the profile, update the profile photo and cover image, and respond to new friend requests. Those are the boundaries of what they can do. They cannot log in as you. They cannot read your private messages. They cannot post new content as though they were you. The line between managing a tribute and impersonating a person is clear, and Facebook maintains it.

The alternative to memorialization is deletion. Facebook gives you that choice too, and it is a legitimate one. Some people would rather their profile simply disappear than exist as a permanent online monument. Neither choice is wrong. The point is that you get to make it, right now, before anyone else is in the position of having to make it for you.

To set up either option on Facebook, go to Settings and Privacy, then Settings, then Accounts Center, then Personal Details, then Account Ownership and Control, then Memorialization. The path is longer than it should be, but each step is clearly labeled. The whole thing takes about five minutes. You can designate a Legacy Contact, or you can request that the account be deleted after your death, and Facebook will honor whichever you choose.

What Your Legacy Contact Cannot Do

This is worth dwelling on for a moment, because people sometimes misunderstand the scope of this role.

Your Legacy Contact is not a digital executor in the full

sense. They are not stepping into your account and conducting your affairs on your behalf. They are a caretaker of a memorial, not an operator of an account. The distinction matters because some people assume that naming a Legacy Contact solves the problem of accessing everything on Facebook. It does not.

The private messages in your Facebook inbox are not accessible to your Legacy Contact. The data that Facebook holds about you, your browsing activity, your ad targeting profile, your location history, none of that becomes available. The personal information that Facebook considers private stays private. If a family member needs access to that kind of data for legal or estate purposes, the process is more complicated and involves submitting formal documentation to Meta.

For most families, the Legacy Contact arrangement is exactly what they actually need. They want to be able to post a farewell message on behalf of the family, keep the profile visible as a place where friends can leave remembrances, and have someone with the ability to make a few basic decisions about how the profile looks. That is what the Legacy Contact role is designed for, and it handles that job well.

What it does not do is solve the account access problem for anything beyond those specific functions. That problem requires the tools covered in Chapter Three.

Google: The Account That Knows the Most

Your Google account works differently from every other platform in this chapter. There is no memorial mode and no public-facing profile for friends to visit. What Google offers instead is Inactive Account Manager, a tool that lets you decide in advance who gets access to your Gmail,

Google Photos, or Google Drive, and when. Chapter Three covers the full setup. If you haven't configured it yet, that's where to go.

Apple and the Social Layer

Apple doesn't have a social platform, but it's worth a brief mention here because iMessage is how many people in this age group stay in closest contact with their families. If you've had years of meaningful exchanges through iMessage, those conversations are stored in iCloud if you have iCloud backup turned on. Your Apple Legacy Contact, covered in Chapter Three, can access them. Whether you want that to happen is worth deciding when you choose who to designate.

Instagram: The Platform That's Catching Up

Instagram's approach to account management after death has historically lagged behind Facebook's, which is notable given that both platforms belong to the same company, Meta.

For most of Instagram's existence, the only option available to a family after a death was to request that the account be memorialized by submitting a form with proof of death. A memorialized Instagram account preserves the profile and all its posts, but no one can log into it. The photos stay visible. The account is essentially frozen. There was no Legacy Contact, no one authorized to make decisions about the profile on the family's behalf.

Instagram still has no Legacy Contact feature. Unlike Facebook, Instagram has not built any mechanism that lets you designate someone in advance to manage your profile. When you die, your family's only options are to request memorialization or request deletion, both of which require submitting proof of death and your relationship to the deceased. No one can log into the account or download the photo archive on your behalf. That last point is the one that matters most for your photos: the time to get them out is now, not after something happens.

In the meantime, the practical advice for Instagram is the same as it has been: if you have photos on Instagram that matter to you and exist nowhere else, download your data now. Instagram, like Facebook, has a tool that lets you export everything you have posted. In your Instagram settings, look for Your Activity, then Download Your Information, and follow the prompts. The resulting file will include every photo and video you have posted, along with your messages and other account data. Save that file somewhere your family can find it, and make a note of it in the account inventory you built in Chapter Two.

Do not rely on Instagram as your primary photo archive. The memorialization process preserves visibility, but it does not give your family a way to download your library after the fact. The time to get your photos out is while you are here to do it.

LinkedIn and the Professional Record

LinkedIn occupies a different emotional register than Facebook or Instagram, but it deserves a mention because it is where a significant portion of people in this age group have documented their professional lives.

A LinkedIn profile often represents decades of work history, professional relationships, recommendations written by colleagues and managers, and a record of accomplishments that has no equivalent anywhere else. For some families, the idea of that profile simply sitting there indefinitely, or disappearing without notice, is genuinely uncomfortable.

LinkedIn offers two paths after a death, and which one is available to you depends on your legal relationship to the deceased. If you are an executor or court-appointed estate representative, you can request either full account closure or memorialization by submitting LinkedIn's deceased member request form. That process requires the member's full name, profile URL, date of death, a death certificate, and legal documentation establishing your authority, typically letters testamentary or letters of administration. LinkedIn is explicit that a will, power of attorney, or birth certificate is not sufficient for a closure request.

If you are a family member without that legal standing, you can still request memorialization, which locks the profile, prevents new activity, and preserves it as a static professional record. That process requires the member's name, profile link, your relationship, and a link to an obituary or similar proof of death. LinkedIn will not provide login credentials to anyone, and accounts are non-transferable. The platform does not currently offer a proactive Legacy Contact feature the way Facebook does. You cannot designate someone in advance who will be authorized to manage the profile after you are gone.

What you can do is leave instructions. If you have a preference, whether you want the profile memorialized as a lasting professional record or removed entirely, note that preference somewhere your family will find it. The inventory document from Chapter Two is the right place. A simple line saying "LinkedIn: please have this removed after I die, the login is in my password manager" is enough to spare your family a decision they'd rather not make on their own.

LinkedIn is also worth thinking about from a legacy perspective for anyone who built a career that mattered to them. The recommendations on your profile, the endorsements, the record of what you accomplished and who you worked with, that is a document of a life. Some families want to preserve it. Some would rather let it go. Neither is the wrong answer. But it should be your answer, not one made by default.

Twitter, TikTok, and the Platforms You Might Not Think Of

If you are on Twitter, now called X, the platform currently allows family members to deactivate or remove an account after a death by submitting a request with proof. There is no memorial mode and no legacy contact feature. An unaddressed Twitter account simply stays active indefinitely, sending no automatic birthday reminders but remaining visible and searchable.

TikTok is increasingly relevant for people who have been drawn into it through their grandchildren or through the platform's surprisingly broad reach. TikTok does not currently have a legacy contact feature. Family members can request removal of an account after a death, but as with Twitter, there is no proactive planning mechanism available. If you use TikTok and have posted content that matters to you, download it through the platform's data export feature before you need to.

Pinterest, which a significant number of people in this age group use actively, allows family members to close an account after a death by contacting support. There is no public memorial option and no legacy contact feature. If your Pinterest boards represent years of collected recipes, travel ideas, gardening plans, or creative projects, export or photograph the content that matters and save it somewhere outside the platform.

The pattern across all of these smaller platforms is

consistent: they are not as far along as Facebook and Google in building proactive planning tools. What they all have in common is a process for family members to request removal after the fact, and a gap between what is possible with planning and what is possible without it.

The Accounts You Don't Think of as Social Media

There is one more category worth naming, because it tends to surprise people when they realize it applies to them.

Online communities. Forums. Hobby groups. The neighborhood watch group on Nextdoor. The church communication platform. The genealogy site where you have been corresponding with distant cousins for years. The group text in WhatsApp that includes your siblings. The Discord server your grandchildren invited you into. None of these feel like social media in the Facebook sense, but they are all platforms where you have a presence and possibly years of meaningful communication.

Vincent had been a member of a model railroad forum for eleven years. He posted regularly, helped newcomers with technical questions, and had built real friendships with members he had never met in person. When Vincent died, his family had no idea the forum existed. His account stayed active for months, and members who knew him only online were left to wonder what had happened to him. Several sent messages that were never answered. One of them eventually found Vincent's obituary through a Google search and posted it in the forum. Other members replied with things about Vincent, stories and gratitude and fond descriptions of his patience as a teacher, that his family would never see.

This is not primarily a security problem or an account access problem. It is a human one. The people who knew Vincent in that community had no way to grieve him, and

Vincent's family had no way to know that a community existed that might want to.

When you build your account inventory, do not limit it to the platforms with household names. Include the forums, the communities, the groups, the hobby sites. Note that they exist, and leave your family some sense of what you did there and who you knew. A single paragraph in your estate documents is enough to open a door your family would otherwise never find.

The Problem With Other People's Feeds

There is a dimension of social media after death that most people never think about until it happens to them, and it has nothing to do with their own profile page.

When a platform surfaces an old post or a memory, it doesn't just show up on the deceased person's profile. It appears in the feeds of everyone who was connected to that person. A friend who lives across the country, someone who hadn't heard the news, might have that person's content appear in their daily scroll weeks or months after the death. Not because they went looking for it. Because an algorithm decided it was engaging.

A family member who has worked hard to reach a kind of equilibrium, as much as anyone ever does, can encounter a video or a photo from a deceased loved one not on that person's profile but in their own daily scroll. Promoted by a system that has no idea anything has changed. That experience is different from choosing to visit a memorial page. There is no bracing for it. It simply arrives.

This is part of what gives the account management question its real stakes. Your presence on a social platform doesn't only exist on your profile. It exists in the networks you touched, in the connections and reactions and shared posts that link your content to other people's lives. The platform doesn't contain you. It contains a web of associations, and that web stays active until someone changes its status.

Setting up memorialization sooner rather than later after a death reduces the window during which this kind of unexpected contact can happen. Once an account is memorialized, the platform's automated promotion stops. The account no longer feeds content into other people's streams. It becomes a place you go to, not a place that comes to you.

That distinction matters. Grief is hard enough without the feed deciding when it's time to remember someone.

What To Do When It's Already Too Late

This chapter has been aimed at people who still have time to set things up. But not everyone reading it is in that position. Some people reading this chapter are managing the aftermath of a loss right now, trying to figure out what to do with the social media accounts of someone who left no instructions.

The process is slower and more uncertain without advance planning, but it is not hopeless.

For Facebook, the starting point is the memorialization request form, which you can find by searching "Facebook memorialization request" in any browser. You will need to provide proof of your relationship to the deceased and proof of death. Facebook reviews these requests and typically processes them within a few days to a few weeks. If you want the account deleted rather than memorialized, there is a separate form for that, called a Special Request for a Deceased Person's Account.

For Google, the process for family members without

advance setup is more involved and less predictable. Google will not provide passwords or login access to anyone. Immediate family or legal representatives can submit a request for specific data through Google's deceased user support page, but the outcome depends on the circumstances and the documentation provided. It is slower and less certain than Facebook's process, which is exactly why Inactive Account Manager is worth setting up before it is needed.

For Apple, the path without a Legacy Contact already in place is the hardest of the three. Access typically requires legal documentation including a court order, and the process can take months without a guaranteed outcome. The Apple support page for deceased users is the starting point, and an estate attorney can help with the documentation side.

For every other platform, the general answer is the same: search the platform's help center for terms like "deceased user," "account removal," or "memorial request." Every major platform has some version of this process. None of them are fast. All of them require documentation. And all of them are harder than setting things up in advance would have been.

If you are managing this for someone else right now, be patient with yourself. You are doing something genuinely difficult during an already difficult time, and the platforms were not designed with your situation in mind. Take it one account at a time.

Ask Before You Name Someone

Before you complete any of the platform setups in this chapter, make sure the person you plan to designate knows you're doing it. A Legacy Contact who has never heard the term, or who has no idea they've been named, is not a plan. Most people will say yes immediately when asked. Chapter Seven covers the broader family conversation in full, but this particular ask is narrow enough to make now, before you finish the setup.

A Note on What You're Actually Deciding

Underneath all of the platform settings and process steps, this chapter is asking you to make a few decisions that are worth naming plainly.

The first is what you want your social presence to look like after you are gone. Do you want your Facebook profile to remain as a place where friends and family can gather and remember you? Or would you rather it disappear? Both are legitimate choices. Most people, when they actually think about it, have a clear preference. The platform settings exist to honor that preference.

The second is who you trust to carry out those wishes. Your Legacy Contact on Facebook, your trusted contacts in Google, the person you designate for emergency access in your password manager, these are acts of trust. They are also acts of care for the people you name, because being given clear authority and clear instructions is a far gentler experience than being left to guess.

The third is what you want the record of your online life to say about you. Not in a vain sense. In the sense that your social media accounts, across all the platforms where you have had a presence, contain a record of your interests, your friendships, your sense of humor, your enthusiasms, the things you found worth sharing. That record will outlast you for some period of time. What happens to it is, to a meaningful degree, up to you.

What Staying Up Can Mean for the People Left Behind

This chapter has spent a fair amount of time on what can go wrong when accounts are left unmanaged. That's worth knowing. But it is not the whole picture, and being honest about the whole picture matters here.

Research on grief and digital memorials consistently finds that many bereaved people derive real comfort from a memorialized profile. They post on the person's wall on birthdays. They scroll through old photos. They read the comments other people left, discovering sides of their loved one they hadn't known, or simply feeling less alone in the loss. For some families, a memorialized Facebook profile functions as a gathering place that has no physical equivalent. There is no plaque on a bench, no grave everyone can visit, no physical object that holds the shape of that person's presence in the world. The profile can hold some of that.

Carol's husband James died two and a half years ago. His Facebook profile has been memorialized since the week after his funeral. She visits it occasionally, not compulsively, but when she wants to. She has posted on it twice, once on what would have been their fortieth anniversary and once when their granddaughter was born. "It's not like he can read it," she said. "But writing it out helps. And his friends have left things there that I read sometimes. It's a record of the person he was to people outside our family. I didn't know all of it when he was alive."

The point is that the "right" answer here is not automatically deletion. Some people assume it is, because deletion seems clean and definitive, the kind of thing an organized person would choose. But for many families, a well-managed memorial profile serves their grief rather than extending it. It gives them a place to go that holds something real.

The choice between deletion and memorialization depends on the family you have and the kind of people in it. Some families would find a permanent online presence comforting. Others would find it harder to move through grief with the profile still there. Neither reaction is wrong. The question to ask yourself is not which option seems less complicated but which one actually fits the people who will be left to live with it.

If you are not sure, talk to the people closest to you before you finalize the setting. The family conversation in Chapter Seven is the right place to work through a question like this. But even an informal exchange, asking your adult children or your closest sibling what they would want, can give you a clearer sense of which choice you are actually making and who you are making it for.

Noreen eventually called Facebook and had Martin's account memorialized. It took her almost a year to do it, partly because grief moves slowly and partly because she wasn't sure what she wanted. When it was done, the birthday reminders stopped. The memory posts stopped. The account was still there, but it was quiet in the way a memorial should be quiet.

She told her daughter afterward that she wished Martin had set it up himself. Not because it was hard to do, it wasn't particularly, but because having his wishes in writing would have meant she didn't have to guess. She would have known she was honoring what he wanted, not just making the decision that seemed right to her.

That is the gift this chapter is asking you to give your family. Not a complicated technical setup. Just a clear set of choices, made in advance, that spares the people who love you from having to make them alone.

What To Do This Week

Start with Facebook this week, because it has the most complete set of tools and the most straightforward setup. Go to Settings and Privacy, then Settings, then Accounts Center, then Personal Details, then Account Ownership and Control, then Memorialization. Designate a Legacy Contact if you have someone in mind, or choose the deletion option if that is your preference. If you are not sure yet, simply locate the setting and note where it is. Knowing where the control lives is half the work.

If you use Instagram, go into your settings and download your data. Look under Your Activity for the Download Your Information option. Save the resulting file somewhere your family can find it, such as the shared folder you set up in Chapter Four, and make a note of where it is in your account inventory. Do not leave years of photos stored only on a platform that offers no proactive legacy tools.

Finally, take ten minutes to write a short paragraph for each social media platform you use, describing what you want done with it after you die. Keep it plain. "Memorialize my Facebook account and leave it up" is a complete sentence. "Delete my Instagram entirely" is another. Put that note somewhere your family will find it, whether that's a folder on your computer, a printed page with your estate documents, or wherever you keep other important papers. Tell at least one person it exists. The technical setup and the human communication work together. One without the other is half a plan.

CHAPTER SIX

THE FINANCIAL FREEZE: KEEPING YOUR MONEY ACCESSIBLE WHEN YOU CAN'T

The money is there.
Getting to it is the problem nobody saw coming.

Linda was sixty-one years old and had handled difficult things before. She had been through a contentious divorce, raised two kids mostly on her own through the lean years, and built a career in healthcare administration that required her to stay composed when everything around her was falling apart. When her husband Howard died of a sudden cardiac event on a Wednesday morning in October, she was devastated, but she was not the kind of person who falls apart.

What she was not prepared for was the checking account.

Howard had managed the household finances. Not because Linda couldn't have, but because that was simply how they had divided things over thirty years of marriage. He paid the bills. He managed the investments. He handled the tax accountant. Linda knew they were comfortable. She knew the name of their bank. She did not know the online login, the account number, or whether she was named on the account at all.

The bank froze it three days after Howard died, once the death certificate was filed. The mortgage was set to autopay from that account on the fifteenth. So was the electric bill. So was the car insurance. Linda found out the mortgage payment had bounced when she received a letter from the lender ten days later. She was not in default yet. She was in a grace period. But she was standing in her kitchen holding a letter that said her mortgage hadn't been paid, and the money to pay it was sitting in an account she couldn't touch.

It took eleven weeks and two court appearances before Linda had full access to the account. By the time it was over, she had paid late fees, spent seventeen hours on hold with various financial institutions, and hired a paralegal to help her with the probate paperwork she didn't know she'd need. Howard had left a will. He had named her as his heir. None of that mattered at the bank counter without the right legal authority in hand.

This chapter is about making sure that doesn't happen to your family. The financial piece of your digital estate is where the stakes are most concrete and where the right preparation makes the most immediate difference. And the good news, which I want to get to quickly because it's genuinely good, is that most of this is fixable with steps that take an afternoon, not months.

Why Banks Freeze Accounts and What That Actually Means

When a bank learns that an account holder has died, freezing the account is standard procedure. This is not cruelty and it is not a bureaucratic mistake. It is the bank protecting the estate from fraudulent withdrawals while the legal process sorts out who is authorized to receive what. The bank has no way of knowing, in the immediate aftermath of a death, who has legitimate authority over the account. Until someone produces documentation proving they do, the account goes nowhere.

The freeze applies to individual accounts. Joint accounts work differently. If your checking account has two names on it and your spouse or co-owner is one of them, the surviving owner typically retains access without interruption. The account is theirs as much as it is yours. The bank does not freeze it when one owner dies.

But individual accounts, accounts held in your name alone, are the ones that get locked. And for people who manage their finances independently, whether by habit or by necessity, that can mean every bill connected to that account suddenly has no path to payment.

The legal process for getting access varies. In some cases a surviving spouse can present a death certificate and be granted access relatively quickly, particularly for smaller accounts. In others, the estate has to go through probate before any financial institution will release funds to anyone. Probate is the court-supervised process for distributing a deceased person's assets, and while it is a functioning legal system, it is not fast. Depending on the circumstances, it can take months or longer. The money is not gone. It is simply inaccessible while the wheels turn.

None of this has to be your family's experience. The tools for preventing it are straightforward and available right now. You just have to use them.

The Single Most Important Fix: Beneficiary Designations

Here is the thing about financial accounts and probate that

most people don't fully understand until someone explains it plainly: a named beneficiary bypasses the entire system.

When you name a beneficiary on a bank account, you are creating what's called a payable-on-death designation, usually abbreviated as POD. It is a simple form your bank will give you if you ask for one. You fill in a name. You sign it. The bank attaches it to your account. And from that moment on, that account exists outside the probate process entirely. When you die, your beneficiary walks into the bank with a death certificate and a valid ID. In most cases the bank verifies the documentation and transfers the account with minimal delay. No probate required, no court, no legal fees eating into the balance. The process varies somewhat by institution and state, but a named beneficiary consistently moves faster and with less friction than any other path.

Investment and brokerage accounts use a slightly different version of the same mechanism, typically called a transfer-on-death designation, abbreviated TOD. The function is identical. A named beneficiary presents a death certificate and receives the assets directly. The securities and funds transfer outside of probate, which means your family has access to that money while they are also managing the grief, the funeral, the paperwork, and every other thing that arrives at once when someone dies.

Retirement accounts, including IRAs and 401(k)s, have their own beneficiary designation system that you set up through the plan itself rather than through the bank. These designations were built into the structure of retirement accounts from the beginning, largely for tax reasons, and they are among the strongest beneficiary protections in all of estate planning. If you have a retirement account with a named beneficiary, that account will transfer to that person with minimal friction. If you have a retirement account with no named beneficiary, or with a beneficiary who died before you and whose designation was never updated, the account goes into your estate and enters the probate process. That distinction alone is a reason to check your designations today rather than next month.

Life insurance and annuities work the same way. Named beneficiary means direct transfer. No beneficiary, or a beneficiary who has died and not been updated, means the proceeds route through your estate. It sounds like a detail. It is not.

The Uncomfortable Reality About Checking These

Most people who have been paying attention to their finances assume their beneficiary designations are in order. Many of them are wrong.

This is not a character flaw. It is a function of time and change. You may have named a beneficiary on a retirement account twenty years ago, when your circumstances were different. You may have named a parent who has since died. You may have designated a former spouse in a designation that predates a divorce. You may have opened an investment account at a new firm after a job change and simply never gotten around to filling out the beneficiary section.

Financial planners see this constantly. The beneficiary form from 1998 still on file. The IRA that names a person who died in 2011. The brokerage account from a rollover that has no beneficiary at all because the form seemed optional when everything was already overwhelming.

None of this is irreversible. Changing a beneficiary designation is almost always simple. You call or log in to your account. You ask for the form or find it in the settings.

You fill it in. You confirm it. Done. The old designation is replaced. The account now routes to the right person.

What is required is actually doing it. Which means knowing it needs to be done. Which is why, right now, before you close this book and go make dinner, this is worth putting on your list for this week.

Joint Accounts: The Simpler Solution That Isn't Always Simple

The other clean solution for bank account access is to have a joint owner on the account. A joint owner is not a beneficiary. They are a co-equal owner. They can access the account any time, not just after you die. Their name is on the account the same as yours. If you die, they continue as the sole owner. The account never freezes for them.

For married couples, this is often the natural setup already. Many couples have had joint checking accounts for decades. If you are in that situation, the checking account problem may already be solved. What is worth verifying is whether any individual accounts exist that your spouse does not have access to, and whether any investment accounts were set up in one name only.

For people who are not in a couple, the joint account approach is more complicated. Adding an adult child as a joint owner on your bank account gives that child full access to the account right now, not just after you die. That is a meaningful amount of trust. It also has potential tax and financial implications. And it can create complications if the joint owner has their own financial difficulties, because a creditor going after your adult child's assets could theoretically have a claim on a joint account.

This is one of those places where I am not going to tell you what to do. Joint ownership is a real option and it works cleanly in many situations. Whether it is the right option for your specific family and financial situation is a conversation worth having with a financial advisor or attorney. What I can tell you is that leaving an individual account with no beneficiary and no joint owner is the worst of the available options, and the one most likely to create the situation Linda found herself in.

The Autopay Problem That Blindsides Every Family

In many households, one spouse handles the finances quietly, and when they're gone, the other discovers a tangle of automatic payments they never knew existed. For financial accounts, the consequences reach further than a few unwanted subscriptions. The bills that matter most, your mortgage, homeowner's insurance, utility accounts that keep a property habitable, car insurance, are the ones with real downstream consequences if they lapse. A missed streaming subscription is an inconvenience. A missed mortgage payment triggers a grace period clock. A lapsed homeowner's insurance policy can void coverage on a property your estate still owns. The financial autopay problem is not about nuisance fees. It is about protecting the assets your family is trying to inherit.

When an individual account freezes, autopay connected to it either bounces or, if the account is not frozen immediately, continues pulling until the estate runs dry. Either way your executor needs to act fast on essential financial bills, and they cannot act on what they cannot find.

The fix for this is not complicated. It requires a list.

If you worked through Chapter Two, you may already have a version of this list. What you need here is more specific than what that chapter asked for, because this one is written for someone else to use under pressure, not for yourself. Sit down, look at the last few months of statements from every account that has autopay set up, and make a written record of what you find. The company name. The amount. The account or card it draws from. The date it typically processes. Whether the service is essential to the property, like heat, electricity, or a home security system, or whether it is a convenience that can be suspended without consequence.

Your executor needs this list. Not eventually. Immediately. In the first days after your death, someone is going to be trying to manage a household while also dealing with everything else that arrives at once. A clear list of what is being paid automatically from which account, and which payments are critical to keep going, is one of the most practical gifts you can leave behind. It belongs in your estate documents, right next to your account inventory. Two pages of notes that could save your family weeks of financial detective work at the worst possible time.

Where to Keep This Information Without Creating Security Problems

This is the tension at the heart of digital financial planning, and it is worth being direct about it.

On one hand, your family needs to be able to find your account information when they need it. On the other hand, if account information is easy for your family to find, it is also potentially easy for the wrong people to find. These two goals pull in opposite directions, and the wrong solution to one creates the other problem.

Let's start with what not to do, because that is the simpler list.

Do not put passwords, account numbers, or financial details in your will. A will becomes a public document when it goes through probate court. Any sensitive information in it is visible to anyone who asks to see the court record. Attorneys who handle estate planning see this mistake often enough that they mention it specifically. Passwords in a will do not stay private. They never have.

Do not store your financial passwords in a plain text document on your desktop, a note on your phone without a lock on it, or a sticky note anywhere near your computer. These are not obscure security risks. They are the first places anyone looks.

The practical options fall into two categories. For financial accounts specifically, a password manager with emergency access solves a concrete problem: your executor needs to reach online banking portals, brokerage accounts, and investment platforms, most of which will send password reset links to an email address your executor may also need help accessing. A password manager with a designated emergency contact, set up with an appropriate waiting period, gives your executor a single point of entry rather than a chain of dead ends. Chapter Three covers how to set this up in full.

The second option is physical: a sealed document stored somewhere specific and secure that your executor knows about. Not taped to the inside of a drawer. Not in an envelope in the back of a filing cabinet without any indication of what it contains. A specifically labeled document, in a location you have told your executor about, updated regularly, that contains your account list, your financial login information, and your autopay list. A safe, a lockbox, or a fire-resistant document bag stored with your other important papers all work. The critical piece is that someone who is authorized to have it knows where it is and knows it exists.

Many families use a combination. The password manager handles the day-to-day security. The physical document is the backup that works even if the technology fails or the emergency access feature isn't set up correctly. Redundancy is not paranoia here. It is good planning.

Your Estate Documents Need to Name a Digital Executor

There is a gap in most people's estate planning that creates a specific kind of problem for financial accounts, and it is worth naming plainly.

A traditional executor has legal authority to manage your estate, pay your debts, and distribute your assets. That authority typically extends to your physical property and your traditional financial accounts. What it does not automatically cover, and what many estate documents never address, is your digital accounts and your online financial presence.

Banks and financial institutions have become increasingly careful about this. A financial institution that receives a request from someone claiming to be an executor, seeking access to an online account, may ask for very specific documentation establishing that the executor has authority over digital assets, not just physical ones. Without that language in the estate documents, the institution has grounds to refuse access even to someone with entirely legitimate standing.

The person you designate as your digital executor, and it can be the same person as your regular executor or a different one, needs language in your estate documents that specifically authorizes them to access, manage, and if necessary close your online accounts. This is not a complicated addition to existing documents. It is a few sentences. But those sentences matter when your executor is sitting across a desk from a bank representative who is looking for explicit authorization to let them in.

If you have not yet had your estate documents reviewed by an attorney, this is worth adding to the list of things to discuss. If you have documents in place that were drafted some time ago, those documents may not include digital asset language at all, simply because it was not on anyone's radar when they were written. A review is worth the time.

The Online-Only Account Problem

There is a category of financial account that creates special challenges for estate planning, and it is a growing one.

Online-only banks, investment apps, and payment platforms operate entirely on the web. There is no branch to walk into. There is no local representative who knew your father. There is no physical presence to visit when you need to sort out an estate matter. Everything happens through the platform, and the process for handling deceased account holders can be slow, rigid, and not designed with grieving families in mind.

The balances on these platforms are easy to forget about because they don't feel like real bank accounts. A PayPal balance from an online sale two years ago. A Venmo balance that never got transferred. A Robinhood account with a few hundred dollars from a casual investment. None of these feel significant until someone dies and the family realizes there is money sitting in an app that no one can access, and the platform needs formal estate documentation before releasing a dollar of it.

To understand what your family would actually face, it helps to know how the largest of these platforms work, and just as importantly, which ones are different enough that they belong in a separate category entirely.

Zelle: The Biggest Platform That Works Differently

Zelle deserves a specific note because it has more enrolled users than any other payment service in the country. Here is the important thing: Zelle does not hold your money. It is a transfer network, not a wallet. Money moves through Zelle directly from one bank account to another, instantly, and then it is gone from Zelle entirely. There is no Zelle balance for your estate to recover. Whatever moved through Zelle is already in your bank account, and your bank account is where your family will need to go. Zelle does not need its own entry on your inventory the way PayPal does, but the bank account behind it does.

PayPal, Venmo, Cash App, and Apple Cash: Where Balances Actually Live

The platforms that genuinely can hold orphaned balances, money sitting in a digital wallet that your family might not know exists, are a specific group. PayPal is the largest of them, with an estimated 186 million American adult users. Venmo, which is owned by PayPal but operates as a separate app with its own balance system, has roughly 100 million users. Cash App has around 57 million monthly users. Apple Cash, the stored-value component of Apple Pay, adds to the picture for iPhone users who have ever received money or kept a balance in their Apple Wallet.

Each of these platforms can hold real money that has no path to your heirs unless your executor knows the account exists and goes through the platform's estate process to claim it.

PayPal is the most structured of the group. The company has a dedicated Deceased Account Team and a documented process. Your executor submits a cover sheet identifying the account by the primary email address associated with it, along with a copy of their government-issued ID, a death certificate, and legal documentation such as a will confirming their authority. PayPal then releases the balance either by check or by transfer to the bank account already linked to the PayPal account, and closes or locks the account. The critical thing to know: PayPal offers no payable-on-death beneficiary designation on any account type. Every PayPal balance goes through the estate process. There is no shortcut.

Venmo handles estate matters through its own support process rather than through PayPal's Deceased Account Team, which might surprise you given that PayPal owns it. Your executor contacts Venmo support directly, submitting a death certificate and documentation of their legal authority. Venmo's process is less structured than PayPal's and tends to require more back-and-forth before the account is resolved. If the deceased also had a Venmo credit card, that is handled separately through a different form focused specifically on the card account.

Cash App has a basic estate services process. Your executor contacts Cash App support and submits a death certificate along with documentation of their legal authority. Like PayPal and Venmo, Cash App offers no beneficiary designation feature, which means every Cash App balance defaults to the estate process. The platform's estate guidance is thinner than PayPal's, so expect the process to require more direct communication with support rather than a straightforward document submission.

Apple Cash is worth mentioning separately from Apple Pay,

because the two are often confused. Apple Pay is a payment method, not a balance. When you tap your phone at a store checkout, Apple Pay is processing a charge against a debit or credit card you have on file. There is nothing stored in Apple Pay itself. Apple Cash is different. It is a stored-value account, a digital wallet balance that lives inside your Apple Wallet. If someone has sent you money through iMessage and you accepted it into Apple Cash rather than transferring it to your bank, that balance is sitting in your Apple Cash account. It is real money that your estate would need to claim, and doing so routes through the Apple Legacy Contact process covered in Chapter Three.

Robinhood occupies a different category from all of the above. It is an investment platform, not a payment app, but it earns a mention here because its accounts can hold real balances and because many people started using it casually during the years when commission-free stock trading became widely available. Robinhood added transfer-on-death beneficiary designations in 2022, which was a significant improvement. If you have a Robinhood account, you can name a TOD beneficiary directly in the app, and that account will transfer outside of probate. An account without a named beneficiary goes through Robinhood's estate process, which requires submitting a death certificate and government ID through their estates form or by email, after which a dedicated estate representative guides the process.

The pattern across all of these platforms is the same: no proactive planning means the estate process, probate documentation, waiting, and back-and-forth. A named beneficiary where the platform offers one, and at minimum a clear account inventory that your executor can use as a roadmap, makes an enormous difference in how quickly any balance gets to where it belongs.

The most important thing you can do right now is make sure these accounts appear in your inventory. Note the platform name, the approximate balance, and the email address and phone number associated with the account, since many platforms use phone verification as part of their identity process. Your executor needs this map. An account nobody knows exists is money that may simply flow to the state's unclaimed property fund, and your family will never see it.

Small Businesses, Side Hustles, and Domain Names

Not everyone who needs to read this chapter has a simple financial life. A lot of people in their sixties and seventies have built something on the side, a small business, a creative venture, a second act after retirement, and that something almost certainly has a digital financial presence that a standard estate checklist will not think to ask about.

An active Etsy shop with a few dozen listings represents real inventory, real revenue, and a real seller reputation built over years. An eBay account with a high feedback rating has genuine value. A PayPal account attached to either of those is a business payment account as much as a personal one, and the balances in it reflect transactions that are still in process when someone dies. These accounts do not close themselves. They keep receiving orders, or they sit in limbo with funds tied up, or they trigger disputes with buyers who received no communication after a purchase. Someone needs to manage the transition, and they need to know where to look.

The same is true for anyone who has sold anything through Facebook Marketplace, Poshmark, Mercari, or any of the other platforms where selling secondhand goods has become a normal part of managing household finances. If money is moving through it, it belongs in your inventory.

Domain names deserve special attention, because the consequences of letting one expire go further than most people realize.

If your family has ever registered a web address, smith-family.com, your name followed by .com, a site for a small business, a memorial page, anything at all, that registration is typically connected to a credit card set to renew automatically every year. When you die and the credit card is canceled, the renewal fails. The domain goes into a grace period, then expires, then becomes available for anyone in the world to register. Once it is gone, it is gone. Registering it again, if it becomes available at all, means starting over from scratch.

That would be an annoyance for a family website. For a family using custom email addresses tied to that domain, it is a genuine crisis.

Custom email addresses built on a personal or small business domain, addresses like paul@wilczynskifamily.com or orders@yourbusiness.com, only work as long as the domain is active. If the domain lapses, those email addresses stop functioning. Mail sent to them bounces. And as Chapter One established, email is the master key to nearly every financial account you own. Password resets, verification codes, bank statements, account alerts: if the executor cannot reach that inbox because the domain expired, every account recovery that runs through that email address becomes significantly harder or impossible.

If you own a domain name, the fix is simple but specific. Log in to wherever the domain is registered, common registrars include GoDaddy, Namecheap, Google Domains, and Squarespace, and make sure your executor knows the account exists, the login credentials are in your inventory, and the renewal card on file is one that will not be immediately canceled after your death. Some registrars allow multi-year renewals, which buys time. Some allow you to lock in auto-renewal with a backup payment method. Any of these is better than a domain that quietly expires while your family is managing everything else.

Add web hosting accounts, domain registrars, Etsy shops, eBay seller accounts, and any other digital storefront to your financial inventory alongside your bank accounts and investment accounts. They may not have the same balances, but in some cases they have more immediate consequences when they go dark.

Cryptocurrency: The Account With No Customer Service

Everything covered in this chapter so far shares one characteristic most people take for granted: if something goes wrong, there is someone to call. A support team. A process. A form to submit. Cryptocurrency held in a private wallet has none of that, and that distinction is not a minor technical detail. It is the difference between a difficult estate problem and a permanent one.

To understand why, you need to know what a seed phrase is. When someone sets up a self-custody cryptocurrency wallet, the wallet generates a seed phrase: typically twelve to twenty-four ordinary words in a specific sequence, something like harbor sunset marble frozen given lantern velvet mirror autumn bridge castle pearl. That sequence is the master key to everything in the wallet. It cannot be reset. It cannot be recovered by a company. It cannot be subpoenaed by a court. If the seed phrase is lost, the cryptocurrency in that wallet is gone. Not transferred. Not locked in probate.

Gone, permanently and irreversibly, with no appeal and no exception.

If you hold cryptocurrency in a self-custody wallet, the seed phrase needs to be written down, stored physically in a secure location, and documented in your estate papers the same way you would document a safe combination or a PIN. It should never be stored only on a computer or phone. Devices fail, get lost, and get wiped. The seed phrase needs to exist on paper or on a purpose-built metal backup plate, in a location your executor knows about and can reach. This is one of the few situations in this book where the stakes of not documenting something are truly absolute.

Cryptocurrency held on an exchange like Coinbase is more manageable. Coinbase has a documented estate process: your executor submits a death certificate, probate documents establishing their authority, a valid government ID, and signed instructions directing Coinbase to transfer the assets. The process exists, the assets are recoverable, and an executor with the right documentation can reach them. The critical requirement is simply that your executor knows the account exists. Coinbase will not send your family a letter after you die. Your inventory should note the exchange name and the email address associated with the account so your executor knows it is worth pursuing. And do not put your seed phrase in your will. A will becomes a public document when it enters probate, and a seed phrase there is an open invitation to anyone who searches the court record. It belongs in a sealed physical document, stored securely, with access limited to the person you trust to handle your estate.

A Conversation Worth Having

Phillip had been a careful man with money his entire

adult life. He had maxed out his 401(k) every year he was employed. He had built up a brokerage account over forty years, never dramatic in its growth, just steady. He and his wife had a joint checking account and had owned their house outright since 2009. By any reasonable measure, he had done the right things.

What he had never done was tell his adult daughter where any of it was.

Not because he was secretive. He was simply, like a lot of people of his generation, of the view that financial matters were his to manage and would get sorted out when the time came. He had a will. His wife was the primary beneficiary on everything. He trusted the system to work.

When Phillip died at seventy-eight, his wife Eleanor was eighty years old and in the early stages of cognitive decline. She knew they had investments but couldn't remember where. She knew there was a brokerage account but not which firm. She knew the checking account number because she had written it on checks for sixty years, but she had never logged into the online portal.

Their daughter Sarah spent four months piecing together a financial picture that should have taken an afternoon. She found accounts by searching through old tax returns and mail. She called financial institutions using only a last name and a rough description of the account type, which did not go well until she had probate documentation in hand. She recovered everything eventually. Nothing was lost. But four months of her life went into a search that a one-page document could have eliminated entirely.

Phillip was a careful man. He just hadn't finished the job.

The financial piece of digital estate planning is not really about technology. It is about finishing the job. The accounts are set up. The assets are there. The will exists. The missing step is usually the one that connects your executor to the information they need to act on everything else you've put in place.

What Happens If You're Incapacitated, Not Dead

This is the piece that often gets left out of estate planning conversations, and it matters every bit as much as what happens after death.

If you have a stroke, a serious fall, a medical event that leaves you hospitalized and unable to manage your own affairs for weeks or months, your family has a different kind of access problem. They need to pay your bills. They need to check your accounts. They need to manage your finances while you are alive but unable to do it yourself. Your executor has no authority in that situation. Your estate documents do not apply while you are still here.

What covers this situation is a durable power of attorney for financial matters. A durable power of attorney gives the person you name, typically called your agent, the legal authority to manage your finances on your behalf if you become incapacitated. The word durable is the critical one. A regular power of attorney stops working if you become mentally incapacitated. A durable power of attorney continues working precisely in that situation, which is when you need it most.

If you do not have a durable power of attorney in place and you become incapacitated, your family may need to go to court to establish a guardianship or conservatorship before they can pay your mortgage or access your bank accounts. That process is slow and expensive and emotionally brutal for everyone involved. It is exactly the kind of thing a durable power of attorney is designed to prevent.

This is not something to set up with a form from the internet, or rather, you can try, but the stakes are high enough that it is worth doing with an attorney to make sure it is valid and covers what you need it to cover. If you have estate documents in place and have not revisited them recently, check whether a durable power of attorney is included. If it is not, this is the most urgent addition to make.

The Retirement Account That Was Never Updated

One of the most consistent and costly mistakes in financial estate planning is the retirement account beneficiary that was set up decades ago and never reviewed.

Connie was sixty-seven when her mother died. Her mother had worked as a nurse for thirty-two years and had contributed to a 403(b) retirement account throughout her career. When Connie began the estate process, she found the account. It had a substantial balance. The named beneficiary was her father.

Her father had died nine years before her mother.

The account had no contingent beneficiary, which is the backup beneficiary named in case the primary one has already died. With no living primary beneficiary and no contingent beneficiary, the account defaulted to her mother's estate and entered the probate process. Which meant it was treated as a regular estate asset, which meant significant tax consequences that would not have applied if the account had transferred directly to Connie as a named beneficiary, and which meant waiting through the probate timeline for access.

The money was not lost. But tens of thousands of dollars in avoidable tax consequences landed on the estate simply because a beneficiary form had sat unchanged on file since the 1990s.

Retirement account beneficiary designations should be reviewed every few years as a matter of routine. Any time a major life event happens, a marriage, a divorce, a death in the family, the birth of a grandchild you might want to include, sit down and review who is named on every retirement account you hold. Most institutions let you do this online in ten minutes. It is ten minutes that can prevent exactly the situation Connie found herself in.

The Digital Key to Everything Financial

For most financial institutions, your email address is the password recovery mechanism. Reset links, verification codes, and account statements all route there. An executor who cannot access your email will hit a wall every time they try to get into an online financial account, even with the right credentials in hand. Make sure your inventory notes which email address is tied to which financial account, and make sure your executor has a path to that inbox. Chapter Three covers email access as part of the broader digital access picture.

Gary and the Spreadsheet He Finally Made

Gary was sixty-nine years old and had been a high school history teacher for thirty-four years before retiring. He was the kind of person who knew a great deal about a great many things and had a reputation among former students for being the teacher who made you actually think. He was also, by his own admission, someone who had been putting off getting his financial paperwork in order for about four years.

His daughter had mentioned it twice. His doctor, during a routine conversation about end-of-life preferences, had mentioned it once. Gary had nodded both times and continued not doing it, not because he was irresponsible but because it felt like an enormous task and he couldn't quite see where to start.

What changed it was a conversation with his neighbor, who had spent the previous year managing his wife's estate after her unexpected death. The neighbor was not dramatic about it. He just said, plainly, that the worst parts had not been the grief but the logistics. The weeks of phone calls to institutions that would not talk to him. The forms that required documentation he did not know he needed. The feeling of failing at something practical when he most wanted to do right by his wife.

Gary went home that evening and spent two hours making a spreadsheet. He listed every financial account he had, the institution, the account type, the approximate balance, the login username, and whether it had a named beneficiary. He found two accounts with no beneficiary designation. He found one retirement account still naming his ex-wife from a marriage that had ended twenty-two years earlier.

He updated all three before the week was out. He printed the spreadsheet, sealed it in an envelope, and put it in the fire safe where he kept his other important documents. He sent an email to his daughter telling her the safe existed and where to find it.

The whole thing took about three hours across two evenings. He said later that it had felt, once he actually did it, less like confronting his mortality and more like finally finishing something he had started and left half-done for years.

That is exactly what it is.

What To Do This Week

The first task is to check the beneficiary designation on one retirement account or investment account you hold. Log in or call the institution and ask what name is currently on file as your beneficiary. If it is outdated, if it names someone who has died, or if there is no beneficiary listed at all, request the form to update it this week. This is the single highest-impact action in this entire chapter, and it takes less time than watching the evening news.

The second task is to make your autopay list. Pull up one month of statements from your primary checking account and write down every recurring charge you see. Company name, amount, which account it pulls from. A simple sheet of paper is fine. The goal is not a perfect document. The goal is a starting point your executor can use. Once you have the list, put it with your estate documents or wherever you keep important papers.

The third task is to check whether you have any balances sitting in payment apps. PayPal, Venmo, Cash App, Apple Cash, and any other app where money might live. Look at the balance. If there is one, add the account to your inventory with the email address and phone number on file. If you have a Robinhood account and have not yet named a TOD beneficiary, do that this week in the app. It takes about five minutes and moves that account entirely outside the probate process. You do not need to do anything special for Zelle, since it holds no balance of its own. Whatever moves through Zelle lands in your bank account, and your bank account is already on your inventory.

The fourth task is to confirm that the person who will handle your estate knows the name of every financial institution where you have accounts. Not the passwords. Not the account numbers. Just the names. You can tell them in a five-minute conversation over the phone. That small act of communication eliminates the four-month search that Sarah had to conduct after her father died.

The fifth task, if you have not already done it, is to find out whether your estate documents include a durable power of attorney for financial matters. Look through what you have, or call the attorney who prepared your documents and ask. If you do not have one, make an appointment to address that. It is not optional. It is the document that protects your family in exactly the scenario nobody thinks will happen to them until it does.

If you own cryptocurrency, add one more task: confirm that your seed phrase for any self-custody wallet is written down, stored physically somewhere secure, and known to your executor. Most people reading this do not own crypto, and if that is you, you can skip this one entirely. But if you do hold it, this is the highest-stakes item on the whole list. Chapter Eight covers crypto documentation as part of the broader estate package.

CHAPTER SEVEN

THE CONVERSATION: HOW TO TELL YOUR FAMILY WHAT YOU'VE DONE

Why doing it now is an act of love, not a morbid chore.

Marcus was a planner. His children knew this about him. He had a will. He had life insurance. He had a file cabinet in his home office with labeled folders that his wife called the Command Center. When he retired at sixty-eight, he spent a few weeks getting his digital life in order too—password manager, Legacy Contact set up on his iPhone, beneficiary designations reviewed and updated, the autopay list his daughter would need sitting in an envelope right on top of everything else.

He had done the work. All of it. Every chapter of this book, essentially.

He just never told anybody.

When Marcus had a heart attack at seventy-two and spent six weeks in cardiac rehabilitation, his wife Sylvia found the file cabinet right away. She found the envelope. She found the printed page from his password manager with the emergency access instructions. But she had no idea what any of it meant, because Marcus had never walked her through it.

The Command Center was labeled, but nobody else spoke the language.

It took Sylvia three weeks of phone calls, a visit from their daughter in from Portland, and one genuinely embarrassing conversation with the bank before she was fully back on her feet financially. None of it was Marcus's fault, exactly. He had prepared everything any reasonable person could prepare. He had simply assumed that leaving good documentation was the same as having the conversation. It is not.

This chapter is about the conversation. The one that turns everything you have done in the first six chapters from a private project into a shared plan. It is not a complicated conversation. It does not require an agenda or a conference table or anyone's attorney on the phone. It requires a little honesty, a clear head, and the willingness to say out loud: here is what I have done, here is where it lives, and here is what I want you to do with it if something happens to me.

Why People Put This Off

The practical work of getting organized—the inventory, the password manager, the beneficiary designations—is something people can do alone, at their own pace, without having to discuss mortality with anyone they love. That makes it easier to start. It also makes it easy to declare it finished before the most important part is done.

The conversation is harder because it requires you to say, plainly, that you will not always be here. That is not a comfortable sentence for most people, and it is not a comfortable sentence for the adult children who need to hear it. Research on why older adults avoid these discussions consistently surfaces two fears: the fear of being seen as giving up, and the fear of being seen as a burden. Neither of those things is what a conversation like this means. But feelings are not always logical, and the fear is real.

Studies on advance care planning find that a prior health scare is one of the strongest predictors of whether someone will have these conversations at all. Not planning, not prudence, not love for their family. A scare. People wait until something frightening has already happened before they find the words.

There is also an awkwardness that runs in the other direction. Adult children who want to have this conversation often hold back because they don't want to seem like they're rushing things, or angling for an inheritance, or implying that their parent can no longer manage their own affairs. A 2023 survey found that roughly two-thirds of Americans believe adult children have significant responsibility for helping aging parents, yet the same research makes clear that most families never sit down and work through the practical details. Everyone feels responsible. Almost nobody starts the conversation.

The result is that both sides are waiting for the other to go first. And the conversation never happens.

What usually forces it is a health scare. Someone lands in the hospital. Someone gets a diagnosis. And now the conversation is happening in a waiting room at the worst possible time, under the worst possible conditions, with information that is incomplete and accounts that haven't been organized yet.

Do not wait for the waiting room. That is the whole point of this chapter.

What This Conversation Is Not

Before describing what this conversation should be, it is

worth being clear about what it is not, because people sometimes talk themselves out of having it by imagining it wrong.

It is not a legal proceeding. You are not reading your will aloud. You are not transferring any authority to anyone. Nothing changes legally as a result of the conversation. You remain fully in control of every account, every asset, and every decision.

It is not a confession. You are not disclosing secrets. You are sharing a map you have already drawn so that the right people know where it is.

It is not one conversation you can never revisit. Your situation will change. Accounts will open and close. Passwords will change. Family circumstances will shift. The conversation is the beginning of an ongoing understanding, not a contract you sign once and file away forever.

And it is not about your death, specifically. It is about what happens if something incapacitates you for six weeks, as it did Marcus. It is about what happens if you are traveling and become unreachable for a few days and something at home needs to be managed. It is about the whole range of situations in which someone you trust might need to step in and help, not only the final one.

When you frame it that way, the conversation becomes easier. You are not asking your family to prepare for your death. You are asking them to know enough to help you if you ever need it. Most people find that framing a relief. It turns a conversation about dying into a conversation about being cared for, and those are not the same thing.

Who Needs to Be In the Room

You do not need to assemble the entire family. In most cases, this conversation involves one person, maybe two. Your spouse or partner, if you have one. One trusted adult child, if you have one who is well-positioned to help. A sibling or close friend if your circumstances make that person the right choice.

The person you are looking for has three qualities. First, they are someone you trust completely with sensitive information. This is not the same as the person you love most, though it can be. It is the person who will use what you tell them carefully and appropriately, and who will not let it spill into family conversations at the wrong moment. Second, they are someone who is reachable. If the person you most trust lives across the country or is hard to contact regularly, you may also need someone geographically closer as a practical matter. Third, they are someone who has demonstrated some ability to handle financial and logistical tasks under stress. Not a specialist. Not someone with any particular credential. Just a capable person who can follow instructions and ask for help when they need it.

If your family includes siblings who don't get along, or adult children with competing interests, or old wounds that tend to surface when money is anywhere in the conversation, this is the moment to think carefully about who should know what. The person with the map does not have to be the same as the person who inherits anything. Those roles can be held by different people, and sometimes that is the cleaner arrangement.

The general rule is this: one primary person who knows the full picture, one backup person who knows where to find it. Two people. That is usually sufficient, and it avoids the complexity of managing a committee. If your primary person becomes unavailable—moves, becomes ill, or you have a falling out—you want someone who can step in.

Name them now.

The Senior's Side of the Table

If you are the one who has done the organizing, here is what you need to communicate. Not all at once, not in technical detail, but clearly enough that the right person could act on it.

The first thing they need to know is that a plan exists. This sounds obvious, but it is not. Many people assume their family has some vague awareness that things are organized. They don't. Sylvia did not know the Command Center was a Command Center. She knew it was a filing cabinet. Tell the person directly: I have gotten my digital life in order, and I want to show you where things are.

The second thing they need to know is where the account inventory lives. Chapter Two produced a list of every account you have—email, bank, investment, insurance, subscriptions, everything. Your family does not need to memorize this list. They need to know where it is. One sentence: the account inventory is in this specific place, here is how to find it.

The third thing they need to know is how to access the password manager. Chapter Three covered this in detail, but the version that matters for this conversation is simpler: the master password, or the emergency access instructions, or both. This is the key to the cabinet. Without it, the cabinet is a locked box that does your family no good at all.

The fourth thing is where your legacy access designations are set up. If you have designated someone in Apple's Legacy Contact, Google's Inactive Account Manager, or through your password manager's emergency access feature, the person in this conversation should know that those designations exist and, ideally, know what they cover. The more specific you can be, the better. "I have set up emergency access in Bitwarden and it requires a 48-hour waiting period before you get in" is infinitely more useful than "I think I did something about passwords once."

The fifth thing, and this is the one most people forget, is what you actually want done. Not just where things are, but what your wishes are. Which accounts should be closed promptly. Which ones hold financial assets that need to be transferred. What should happen to your social media profiles—should they be memorialized or deleted? Are there photos, documents, or emails that you want preserved and shared with specific people? The inventory tells your family where things are. The wishes tell them what to do with what they find. Without the wishes, they are left guessing, and guessing in grief is a hard thing to ask of the people who love you.

A word on how much to share. Some people are comfortable walking through their full account list in detail. Others prefer to keep the conversation at a higher level—here is where the inventory is, here is how to access it, here is my attorney's name. Both approaches work. What does not work is leaving it so vague that the person you trust doesn't know where to start. "Everything is organized" is not actionable. "The inventory is in the blue folder in the bottom left desk drawer and the password manager master password is written on the back of the insurance card in the same folder" is actionable.

The Family Member's Side of the Table

If you are an adult child or a trusted person who has been brought into this conversation, your job is simpler than you might expect. It is mainly to listen, to ask clarifying questions where you genuinely need them, and to resist the urge to take over.

That last part deserves emphasis. The purpose of this conversation is for the person who has organized their digital life to hand you a map, not to hand you the wheel. They are still driving. They remain in charge of every account and every decision. What they are giving you is information. Treat it as a gift and a trust, not as an invitation to manage their affairs.

The questions worth asking are practical ones. Where exactly is the inventory? What do I do first if something happens? Is there a person—an attorney, a financial advisor—I should call before I start trying to access things myself? What is the waiting period on the emergency access, and will I get a notification? What do you want me to do with your social media accounts? Is there anything on your phone or computer that you specifically want preserved or specifically want deleted? These are the questions that turn a good conversation into a workable plan.

The questions worth saving for another day are the ones about money, what the accounts hold, who inherits what. Those conversations belong somewhere else, not here.

One thing worth asking permission for: would it be all right if I write down the key points so I can refer to them later? Nobody remembers everything they heard in an emotionally significant conversation. A few notes, taken openly and with permission, are not intrusive. They are practical. They also serve as a record that the conversation happened, which sometimes matters later if questions arise about what was communicated and to whom.

After the conversation, do something with what you were told. Put the key information somewhere you can actually find it. If you were given a copy of the Digital Snapshot, file it with your own important documents. If you learned where the account inventory lives, write that down somewhere it will not get lost in a drawer. Your role here does not end when you walk out the door. You are now a keeper of a plan, and that is a responsibility worth taking seriously.

A Scene Worth Imagining

Ellen is seventy-four and lives alone since her husband died four years ago. Her son David is forty-nine, lives forty minutes away, and calls her every Sunday. He is the person she trusts most, and she has been meaning to have this conversation with him for about two years.

She does not do it on the phone. She asks him to come for lunch on a Saturday. After lunch, before he gets back in his car, she says: "I want to show you something. I've gotten everything organized and I want you to know where it is."

She shows him the account list on her laptop. She shows him how to find the password manager and explains the emergency access waiting period. She shows him the folder in her desk drawer that has her printed account inventory and her wishes written out in plain language. She tells him she has named him as her Legacy Contact on her iPhone and her Google account, and she explains what that means: if her accounts go inactive for three months, he will get a notification and a path to access them. She tells him the name of her attorney and where her estate documents are kept.

The whole thing takes twenty-five minutes.

David does not feel that his mother is preparing to die. He feels that she trusts him, and that she has thought about this carefully. He feels, if anything, relieved. He has been carrying a low-level worry about exactly this for years—not a specific fear, just a background hum of not knowing—and now he has actual information instead of dread.

Ellen feels lighter too. She has been carrying the weight of an incomplete project for two years, and it is done now. Not just organized. Actually done. The work she did across the previous months has finally landed somewhere it can do good.

That is what this conversation feels like when it goes well. Not morbid. Not heavy. Honest, and finished.

What to Do When There Is No Obvious Person

Not everyone has a David. Some people are estranged from their children. Some have outlived their closest friends. Some have family they love but genuinely cannot trust with sensitive financial information—a child with a history of financial problems, a sibling whose discretion has proven unreliable, a family dynamic where sharing this information with one person would immediately create conflict with another. Some are simply private people who have spent their whole lives keeping their financial affairs to themselves, and the idea of handing that information to anyone feels fundamentally wrong.

These are real situations, and they deserve more than a shrug. There are practical options, and while none of them are perfect substitutes for a trusted family member, they are genuine.

An estate planning attorney can serve as the keeper of your plan. You share the location of your account inventory and the emergency access instructions with them, they hold it in a client file, and your executor is instructed to contact the attorney first. This arrangement costs money and requires finding an attorney you trust, but it creates a professional relationship with clear boundaries, appropriate confidentiality, and legal accountability. An attorney cannot misuse your information the way a family member theoretically could. They are bound by professional obligations that private individuals are not.

A trusted friend is a legitimate choice even when it feels unconventional. The question is not whether they are family. The question is whether they are trustworthy, reachable in an emergency, and capable of following instructions. A longtime friend who passes those tests is a better choice than a family member who doesn't. What makes this work is being explicit with the friend about what you are asking them to do, making sure they agree to it, and documenting their role somewhere your other family members will understand. "In an emergency, contact my friend Patricia at this number before doing anything else" is a sentence that can go on the Digital Snapshot described later in this chapter.

A professional fiduciary is an option fewer people know about. A fiduciary is a professional who manages financial and personal affairs on behalf of someone else, typically in situations where family is not available or not appropriate. Not all fiduciaries handle digital estate matters, but the field is evolving quickly, and asking an estate planning attorney whether a professional fiduciary makes sense in your situation is a reasonable question.

Some estate planning services have also begun offering digital estate custodian arrangements, where they hold access information securely until a triggering event—a death certificate, a legal declaration of incapacity—releases it to your designated person. These services vary significantly in quality and in what exactly they hold and how. If this path interests you, scrutinize the terms carefully and ask your attorney to review any agreement before you sign.

Whatever you choose, the goal is the same: at least one person, or one institution, knows that the plan exists and knows how to access it. A plan that is perfectly organized but known only to you is still a wall your family will eventually hit.

When the Conversation Gets Complicated

Most of these conversations go fine. People are relieved to have them. But some do not, and it is worth being prepared for the versions that are harder.

The version where the other person gets defensive. This sometimes happens when an adult child hears "I want to show you where my accounts are" and processes it as "I'm dying" or, worse, as an implication that they have been asking too many questions or pushing too hard. If that defensiveness appears, the most useful response is to slow down and name what you are doing plainly. You are not preparing to die. You are organizing your affairs the same way you have homeowner's insurance and a doctor you see regularly. This is that kind of practical. You are not writing a eulogy. You are making a plan. Those are different things.

The version where the parent resists. If you are an adult child and the person you need to have this conversation with won't engage, a direct approach often makes things worse. What tends to work better is a smaller one. Instead of asking about the whole picture, ask about one thing. "Dad, do you have a folder somewhere with your insurance information? I just want to know where to look if I ever need it." Most people can answer that question. Once they have, the next one is a little easier. You are not trying to extract a complete accounting in one sitting. You are trying to establish that it is safe to talk about this at all. That takes time, and it takes patience, but it is not impossible. If you find a moment when your parent seems open, follow their lead. Don't push past the point where they are comfortable. A small conversation that ends well is worth more than a thorough one that ends badly.

The version where siblings are in the picture. If you have more than one adult child and you are designating one of them as the primary person who knows your plan, the others may have feelings about that. This is worth thinking through in advance. One option is to bring everyone into a joint conversation so they all hear the same information at the same time, which removes any sense of favoritism or secrecy. Another option is to be clear, to everyone, that the person who holds the operational details is not the person who inherits more. Access to information is a practical arrangement. It is not a statement about who you love or trust more. Say that plainly, and repeat it if necessary.

Old family dynamics have a way of showing up in conversations like this. Siblings who have been navigating old roles and old resentments for decades do not suddenly set all of that aside because the topic is practical. The Family Caregiver Alliance, which has studied sibling dynamics in caregiving situations extensively, notes that old rivalries and past roles tend to resurface under exactly the kind of stress these conversations can generate. You cannot fully prevent that. What you can do is make your intentions clear enough that there is less room for misinterpretation. The more specific and documented your wishes are, the less space there is for conflict to fill.

The version where the conversation surfaces something you didn't expect. Sometimes a conversation that starts with digital accounts ends up somewhere more personal. A family member says something that reveals how much worry they have been carrying. Or you find yourself saying something about your wishes that you hadn't fully articulated before. This is not a problem. It is the conversation working the way it is supposed to. Let it go where it needs to go. The practical details will still be there when you come back to them.

The Digital Snapshot Your Family Needs

One of the most practical things you can do before this conversation is prepare a single page your family member can take with them when they leave. Not a binder. Not a manual. One page.

Call it whatever makes sense to you. Digital Summary for My Family. Emergency Information. What You Need to Know First. The name does not matter. What matters is that it contains the essential information a trusted person would need in the first twenty-four hours of an emergency, without requiring them to already know where everything is.

Here is what belongs on that page. Where the account inventory lives—the specific location, whether that is a folder in a filing cabinet, a document on a computer, or a printed sheet in a lockbox. How to initiate emergency access on your password manager—the name of the app, the name of the trusted contact who is already designated, and the waiting period they should expect. The name and phone number of your attorney. The location of your physical estate documents—your will, your power of attorney, any advance directive. The name of your financial advisor, if you have one. And your key wishes for your digital accounts: which social media profiles you want memorialized or deleted, who should receive access to your photos, whether there are any accounts that hold financial value and need to be handled promptly.

Notice what is not on that page: actual passwords. This is not a password list. It is a map to the map. If your password manager and your legacy contact designations are set up correctly, your trusted person does not need your passwords written on a piece of paper. They need to know where to find them and how to access them when the time comes. Passwords on paper create security risks. A map to the password manager does not.

Keep this document updated. If you change your attorney, update the page. If you move your account inventory to a different location, update the page. If you change the master password on your password manager, update the page. An outdated map is almost as unhelpful as no map at all.

Put it somewhere physical that your designated person can find. You'll settle on the exact location when you assemble everything in Chapter Eight. Tell them it exists and tell them where it is. A document no one can find is no better than no document at all.

Revisiting the Conversation

This is not a one-time event. The conversation you have today reflects your situation today. A year from now, some of that will have changed, and your trusted person will be working from an outdated picture unless you bring them up to date.

A reasonable rhythm is once a year, at a time that is easy to remember. Some people tie it to their insurance review in January. Some do it when they file their taxes. Some use a birthday—their own, a spouse's, or a child's—as a standing annual prompt. The specific timing matters less than the habit of doing it.

Some changes warrant a conversation sooner than the annual review. A death in the family, especially if the person who died was named as a beneficiary or a trusted contact in your plan, requires an immediate update. A divorce—your own or an adult child's—can change who should have access to what. A major health event, your own or your designated person's, is reason to sit down and review whether the current plan still makes sense. A significant financial change, like selling a property or opening a new investment account, means the inventory needs updating and your designated person needs to know. And if you have a falling out with the person you designated, you need to change the designation and have the conversation with someone new. A plan that routes to the wrong person is worse than no plan at all.

Updating is not a failure. It does not mean the original plan was inadequate. It means your life kept moving, which is the whole point. Revisiting this annually is evidence that you took the whole thing seriously enough to maintain it, not just to start it.

The annual conversation does not have to be a formal sit-down. For most people, once the initial conversation has happened and the foundation is in place, the updates are simpler. A phone call: "I wanted to let you know I added a new brokerage account—it's on the inventory now and the login is in the password manager." A note with the Digital Snapshot: "Updated in March 2026." The relationship is already established. The map already exists. You are just keeping it current.

What To Do This Week

Choose one person. Think about who the right person is for your situation. Not every detail of what you will say to them. Just the name. Write it down somewhere you will see it. If you already know, good. If you are not sure, let yourself sit with it for a few days. The answer usually becomes clear. Once you have the name, reach out and ask if they can get together soon. You do not have to explain why in the message. Just get it on the calendar.

Prepare your Digital Snapshot this week. One page: who to call first, where the account inventory and estate documents live, how to initiate emergency access on your password manager, your attorney's name and number, and your key wishes for your digital accounts. It does not need to be polished. It needs to be clear enough that someone who found it in your desk could follow it. When it's done, tell your designated person it exists and where it is.

Have the conversation. When you sit down together, start simply. You do not need an opening speech. "I've gotten my digital accounts organized and I want to show you where things are" is enough. Walk them through what you prepared. Answer their questions. Let them take notes. When it is done, you will both feel better than you did before it. That feeling is the reward for doing the work.

After the conversation, confirm that your trusted person knows where the Digital Snapshot is. That one exchange transforms a private document into an actual plan.

CHAPTER EIGHT

THE "FOR MY FAMILY" PACKAGE: BRINGING IT ALL TOGETHER

You have done the thinking.
Now comes the part that makes it real—
one clear package your family can actually use.

There is a moment that happens when you finish something like this.

It is not a dramatic moment. There are no balloons. You do not feel a wave of accomplishment wash over you while soft music plays in the background. What actually happens is quieter than that. You close a folder, or you slide a notebook into a drawer, or you save a file with a name that finally makes sense. And somewhere in the back of your mind a thought surfaces, small and certain: they will know what to do.

That thought is the whole point of this book.

Not the spreadsheets. Not the platform policies. Not the difference between a legacy contact and an inactive account manager. Those things matter, and we have covered all of them. But they were never the destination. The destination is that quiet moment when you know, without having to convince yourself, that the people you love will not be standing in a hallway three days after your death trying to figure out your email password while also planning a funeral.

This chapter is about getting you to that moment.

The stakes are not hypothetical. A study of professional inheritance advisers in the United Kingdom found that nearly one in four had worked with clients who had already run into serious trouble trying to access a deceased family member's digital accounts. Locked out of photos. Unable to reach financial records. Cut off from email histories that held information nobody thought to write down anywhere else. And that number almost certainly understates the real frequency, because many families never discover all of the accounts the person held, so the problems go unrecorded entirely.

What the First Seven Chapters Actually Did

You have inventoried your accounts, secured access for your trusted people, protected your photos, addressed your financial accounts, and made decisions about your online presence.

That is the foundation. What this chapter gives you is the assembly. Everything you have thought about and decided and noted along the way is about to become a single organized package that another person could actually use. That is a meaningful shift, and it is closer than it probably feels.

Why a Package and Not Just a List

There is a difference between having information and having a package.

Information is scattered. It lives in notebooks and apps and the notes section of your phone and that yellow legal pad you used two years ago when you first started thinking about this. Information requires someone to search for it, interpret it, and figure out what to do with it under conditions of grief and time pressure. That is an unfair thing to leave your family.

A package is organized. It has a starting point. It tells someone where to begin, who to call, what not to do, and where to find the rest. It assumes the person reading it has never thought about any of this before and may be in no condition to think clearly. It does the organizing work in advance so that your family does not have to do it in the worst week of their lives.

The difference between those two things is entirely about how the information is assembled, not about how much information exists. You may already have all the pieces. What this chapter gives you is the assembly.

Think about what a family member actually needs in that first terrible week. They need to know who is the right person to call first, whether that is an executor, an attorney, or simply a trusted person who knows where things are. They need to know where the important documents live. They need to know what accounts exist and roughly what each one contains. They need specific guidance about what not to touch yet, because the list of well-intentioned mistakes a grieving family can make is long. And they need to feel, reading whatever you have left them, that you thought about them when you put this together.

That last part is not sentimental decoration. It is functionally important. A document that feels thoughtful and organized will be used. A document that feels like a data dump will be set aside and probably not returned to until something goes wrong.

One Appointment Is All It Takes to Start

Here is what I want you to do this week. Not this month. Not when things slow down. This week.

Put a single appointment on your calendar. Forty-five minutes. Call it whatever you like. The point of the appointment is not to finish everything. The point is to gather what you already have into one place so you can see what you are working with.

Most people who have gotten this far in the book have more material than they realize. Notes from earlier chapters. Decisions they have already made about platform settings. A list of accounts they started and never finished. Thoughts about what matters most that they wrote down somewhere and promptly forgot about. The appointment is about finding that material and putting it in a single folder, physical or digital, so it stops being scattered.

Forty-five minutes is usually enough to make real progress. You are not writing the package from scratch. You are assembling what already exists. There is a meaningful difference between those two tasks, and the second one is considerably less intimidating than the first.

Before that appointment begins, pull together the things you'll actually need: the account inventory you built in Chapter 2, the Digital Snapshot page from Chapter 7, the emergency access instructions you printed or saved from your password manager, the autopay list from Chapter 6, the name and contact information for your estate attorney if you have one, and any notes you made in earlier chapters about how you want specific platforms handled. You likely have most of this already. The appointment is just the moment you stop letting it live in different drawers and tabs and put it in one place.

The National Institute on Aging, which spends a great deal of time thinking about how older Americans can prepare their families for hard transitions, recommends exactly this approach: put your important papers in one place and make sure a trusted person knows where that place is. The digital version of that advice is the same. One place. One trusted person who knows where it is. That is the minimum viable version of what you are building.

If forty-five minutes once is not enough, schedule a second appointment. And a third if you need it. There is no rule that says this has to happen in a single sitting. What matters is that it happens.

The One Page Your Family Needs Most

In Chapter Seven you built your Digital Snapshot—the one page that tells your family who to call first, where the rest of the information is, and what your key wishes are. That page goes here, at the front of the package, literally on top, so it is the first thing anyone sees. Everything else goes behind it.

The one addition that belongs on the front page and nowhere else: a short list of what no one should do right away. Families make costly and sometimes irreversible mistakes in the first days after a death, almost always with the best intentions. Your list might say: do not close my primary email account until you have reviewed it for important contacts and records. Do not erase my phone or computer before checking what is stored on them. Do not cancel automatic payments until you have a complete list of what I pay and when. Do not guess at account passwords if instructions already exist in this package.

That list is not bureaucratic caution. It is a gift.

The Conversation Your Attorney Needs to Have

If you have a will, a trust, or a power of attorney, this chapter comes with one important piece of additional guidance: your estate attorney needs to know this package exists.

This is not a criticism of your attorney or of the documents they prepared. Wills and powers of attorney are legal instruments, and they are built around the laws that exist when they are written. For most people reading this book, the estate documents they have were prepared before anyone thought carefully about digital assets. The attorney who drew up your will may have done excellent work and still never once discussed what should happen to your Gmail account, your iPhone, your Facebook profile, or the family photos in your cloud storage. That is not negligence. It is a timing issue. Digital estate planning as a recognized discipline is relatively new, and many existing documents simply predate it.

The gap this creates is real. A generic power of attorney that does not specifically address digital assets may leave your designated agent without clear authority to act on your behalf when they try to access an account. A will that does not mention your digital property may leave your executor uncertain about what they are empowered to do. These are not insurmountable problems, but they are problems, and the best time to address them is before they arise.

Your package should include a section that notes the name of your attorney, the name of the firm, a phone number, the date your will was last signed or updated, and a simple reminder that says: ask whether digital assets are covered. That last item is the action item. If your attorney confirms that your existing documents address digital access and your executor's authority, you are in good shape. If they do not, you have identified something worth fixing while you still can.

You do not need to become an expert in estate law to have this conversation. You need to be able to say: I have put together a digital estate plan that covers my online accounts, my devices, my passwords, and my wishes for what happens to my digital presence after I die. I want to make sure my legal documents support that plan. Can we look at whether that is the case?

Most attorneys will be glad you asked.

Building the Package Section by Section

The package itself does not need to be complicated. It does not need to be beautiful. It needs to be organized in a way that makes sense to someone who has never seen it before and may be under significant emotional stress when they open it.

A simple folder with labeled sections is enough. A printed set of pages in a three-ring binder is enough. A clearly organized set of digital files with sensible names is enough. What you are building is not an archive. It is a roadmap. The distinction matters because a roadmap is designed to be followed by someone who does not already know the territory.

Start with your Digital Snapshot page at the front. Behind it, organize the information into logical sections that a family member could move through in order without getting lost.

A section for key people: the executor, the estate attorney, and the person you trust to help with the technical side of things if your family is not comfortable navigating accounts and devices on their own. Include names, roles, and contact information for each.

A section for accounts and bills. This does not need to be exhaustive on the first pass. Start with the accounts that matter most: the primary checking account, any investment or retirement accounts, the accounts tied to recurring automatic payments. Note what each account is, roughly what it contains or what it does, and where to find access information.

A section for devices. List the devices you own, note what is stored on each, and include any relevant access information. This section is particularly important for phones and computers, which tend to hold the most personal and irreplaceable content.

A section for photos, videos, and digital heirlooms. This is the section that carries the most emotional weight for most families. Note where your photos live, whether that is a cloud service, an external drive, a computer, or some combination. If you have taken steps to ensure that a specific person can access your photo library, note what those steps were and what the other person needs to do to claim access.

A section for your major online accounts, with notes about what you have set up in advance. For each tool you configured – Apple Legacy Contact, Google Inactive Account Manager, Facebook memorialization – note who you designated, what they can access, and where the relevant access key or instructions are stored. One or two sentences per tool is enough. The full explanation of each is in Chapters Three and Five.

And at the back of the package, a section for updates and notes. This is where you record the date you last reviewed the package and anything that has changed since the previous version.

The Personal Note Nobody Thinks to Write

Here is something the seed article for this chapter suggested, and I want to give it more room than a passing mention because I think it is genuinely important.

Behind your Digital Snapshot, before you get into the organized sections of the package, include a short personal note for your family.

Not a legal document. Not an instruction sheet. A note.

Tell them what matters most to you in this package. Maybe it is the photos, because the photos are the only place your grandchildren will ever be able to see you at twenty-five. Maybe it is a collection of writing that you have never shared with anyone and that you want them to have. Maybe it is a specific account that holds records they will find useful, or a subscription they should cancel immediately so money stops leaving the bank.

Tell them how you want them to approach this. If you want them to take their time and not feel pressured to handle everything in the first week, say so. If there is something specific they should do first, tell them. If there is something you want them to know about why you put this together, this is the place to say it.

Tell them who should help. If there is a person in your family or circle of friends who is particularly good with technology and would be the right person to sit down with whoever is handling the estate, name that person here. A trusted tech helper can save enormous amounts of time and prevent the kind of well-intentioned fumbling that leads to irreversible mistakes.

This note does not need to be long. Half a page is plenty. But it will almost certainly end up being the most read page in the entire package, because it is the one page that sounds like you.

Where to Keep It and How to Make Sure It's Found

This question sounds simpler than it is. People get it wrong in two opposite directions, and both mistakes have real consequences.

The first mistake is storing the package somewhere so secure that no one can find it when they need it. A safe deposit box is the most common version of this problem. Safe deposit boxes sound like the right answer because they feel official and protected. But in practice, accessing a safe deposit box after a death can require a court order, a waiting period, or the presence of a co-signer who may not be available. That process takes days or weeks, and your family may need the information inside on day two. A package that cannot be reached when it matters most is not much of a package.

The second mistake is leaving it somewhere so accessible that it creates a security risk. A folder sitting on the kitchen counter, visible to anyone who visits, is not the right level of protection for a document that contains account names, access instructions, and the names of financial institutions. Convenience and security pull in opposite directions, and the goal is to find the middle ground between them.

That middle ground looks like a fireproof lockbox or a filing cabinet where you keep other important documents. Something that requires a deliberate effort to open, but is physically present in your home and accessible to the people you trust without requiring legal proceedings. The same physical location where you keep a will, an insurance policy, or a deed is the right place for this package.

A digital copy stored on a shared drive or cloud folder can

be a useful backup, particularly for a family member who does not live nearby. That copy is fine to have. But it should not contain the master password to your password manager. That one piece of information is the exception to every rule about convenience, because whoever holds the master password has access to everything else. It should be shared only through trusted personal communication, a direct conversation with the person who needs it, not stored in any file that could be found, forwarded, or accessed by the wrong person.

The practical test for placement is this: could the person who needs this package most find it without first having to settle the estate? If the answer is yes, you have it in the right place. If the answer is no, move it.

All of that said, the single most important step after assembling the package is telling someone where it is. Not sending them a copy. Not emailing them the contents. Just telling them: there is a folder in the fireproof box in the closet, here is how to open it, and it has everything you will need. That conversation takes two minutes. Without it, even a perfectly organized package can sit undiscovered while your family searches in the wrong places under the worst possible circumstances.

The Mess in the Middle Is Normal

I want to say something directly before we get to the final section, because I have watched enough people go through this process to know that a certain feeling tends to surface right around now.

The feeling is something like: I have done a lot of work and it still feels incomplete.

That feeling is accurate and it is fine.

A digital estate plan is not a thing you finish once and put in a drawer forever. Accounts change. Devices change. The platforms you use change their policies. People you named as contacts or executors move, or their circumstances shift, or your relationship with them changes. Life is not static, and a plan that reflects your life cannot be static either.

What you are building right now is not a perfect permanent document. It is a good-enough current document that is infinitely better than nothing. The difference between a family that finds a thoughtful package in a drawer and a family that finds nothing is not a small difference. It is enormous. It is the difference between a hard week and a catastrophic one.

So if you finish assembling this package and it still has blank sections, loose ends, and things you are not entirely sure about, that is fine. A package with gaps is still a package. Put a date on it and put it somewhere safe and tell someone where it is. Then come back to it when you can.

Which brings us to the annual review.

Set a Date and Come Back Once a Year

Pick one date per year. Thirty minutes. Put it on the calendar now.

The only rule is that the date has to be memorable enough that you will not need a reminder to remember the reminder. The first Sunday of January works well for people who treat the new year as a natural reset. Your birthday works because it is already on the calendar and there is something fitting about spending a few minutes of it thinking about the people you will eventually leave behind. The anniversary of a death that reminded you why this matters is another option, uncomfortable as that sounds.

What you are reviewing each year is straightforward. Have any accounts changed? Have you added a new device? Has the person you named as a legacy contact on any platform moved, died, or become someone you no longer trust with that responsibility? Have any of the platform tools you set up been updated in a way that requires you to revisit your settings? Has your will been updated, and if so, does your attorney know about your digital plan?

Google makes it easy to update your Inactive Account Manager settings at any time through your Google Account. Apple's Legacy Contact designation can be reviewed and changed through the settings on any Apple device. Facebook's memorialization and legacy contact settings are tied entirely to what you set up in advance, so your annual review is the right moment to confirm that those settings still reflect your wishes.

The annual review is also when you update the date on your package. That date matters. When your family opens the package, they will want to know how current it is. A package dated three years ago raises questions. A package dated eight months ago tells them that you were paying attention.

When the Annual Review Can't Wait

The annual cadence works well as a maintenance habit. But certain things that happen in life should send you back to the package before January rolls around, and waiting for the scheduled review when those things occur is not good planning.

A new device is one of them. When you buy a new phone, tablet, or laptop, you are also creating new accounts, new storage locations, and potentially new access issues your family does not know about. The old device you handed to a grandchild or traded in may have held important data you assumed was somewhere else. The new one may be linked to accounts that are not yet in your inventory. Either way, the package is already out of date and you have not made a single purchase yet.

A death or major life change involving someone you named is another trigger that cannot wait. If the person you designated as a legacy contact, emergency contact, or executor has died, moved out of your life, or had a falling-out with the family, that designation needs to be revisited now. The package you built was built around that person. Leaving an outdated name in a critical role is worse than leaving it blank, because it creates the illusion of a plan that no longer functions.

Platform changes are a less obvious trigger but a real one. The major platforms update their legacy tools more often than most people realize. Google has adjusted how its Inactive Account Manager handles data sharing. Apple has changed how Legacy Contact keys are generated and shared. What you set up two years ago may still work, or it may work differently than you think. If you see a news story or a notification about a platform you rely on updating its policies, that is your signal to log in and check.

Significant changes to your accounts also warrant an unscheduled review. Closing a bank you have used for decades, opening a new brokerage or retirement account, canceling a subscription service and starting a different one: each of those moves changes the landscape your family will encounter. The inventory you built in Chapter 2 is only useful if it reflects your actual accounts. A few minutes spent updating it when things change is far easier than reconstructing it from scratch at the annual review.

None of this requires a full review every time something

changes. A targeted update, fifteen minutes at the right moment, is usually enough. The point is simply to recognize the obvious triggers and act on them rather than deferring until January.

What You Have Actually Built

Let me tell you what the package you are assembling represents, because I think it is easy to underestimate it when you are in the middle of putting it together.

You have built a record of your digital life organized specifically for the people who will have to manage it after you cannot. You have thought about what you own in a world where ownership increasingly means accounts rather than objects. You have made decisions about who should have access to what, and you have used the tools available to you to put those decisions into effect. You have considered what your family will need practically and emotionally, and you have tried to give them both.

Most people never do any of this. Not because they do not love their families, and not because they do not understand that it matters. But because it requires sitting with an uncomfortable subject for longer than feels pleasant, and because the sheer scope of modern digital life makes the whole project feel overwhelming before it even begins.

You got past that. That is the actual accomplishment here.

I have a folder in my desk. It is not fancy. It is a manila folder with a label on it that says what it is and the date I last updated it. Inside is a printed document that runs about eight pages. It covers my accounts, my devices, my photos, my wishes for what should happen to my online presence, and the name of my attorney with a note to call her first. My wife knows where it is. So does my daughter.

That folder took me longer to put together than I expected and less time than I feared. The hardest part was starting. Once I started, it turned out to be mostly a matter of writing down things I already knew.

Yours will be the same.

What To Do This Week

Schedule your assembly appointment this week, not this month. A single forty-five-minute block on your calendar is enough to gather what you already have into one place. You are not writing the package from scratch. You are collecting what you have produced through reading this book and giving it a home.

Create your Digital Snapshot page. One page, three sections: who to call first, where the rest of the information is, and what no one should do right away. This page does not need to be long or polished. It needs to be clear. If someone found it in your desk without any context, could they follow it? That is the test.

Write the personal note. Before you organize anything else, write half a page to your family that tells them what matters most to you in this package, how you want them to approach it, and who should help. This is the page they will actually read first, and it may be the most valuable thing in the entire document.

Tell one person where the package is. Before this week is over, tell the person who is most likely to need it first where to find it. Not the whole contents. Just the location. A phone call, a text, a conversation at the kitchen table. That one exchange transforms a private document into an actual plan.

Pick your annual review date and put it on the calendar now. Choose a date you will remember and set a recurring reminder. Thirty minutes once a year is the maintenance cost of a plan that stays current. It is one of the better investments of time you can make for the people who love you.

A FEW TERMS WORTH KNOWING

These terms appear across multiple chapters. This is not a comprehensive glossary of digital estate planning, but a quick reference for the words that come up most often and are not always self-explanatory.

Digital estate

Everything you own or control in digital form: email accounts, cloud storage, social media profiles, online financial accounts, streaming subscriptions, digital photos, and the devices that hold or access all of it. Your digital estate is not separate from your estate in the traditional sense. It is part of it, and it requires its own planning because most of it is governed by platform terms of service rather than property law.

Password manager

An application that stores and organizes your passwords in an encrypted vault, protected by a single master password. Instead of remembering dozens of different passwords, you remember one and the manager handles the rest. Most password managers also generate strong unique passwords for new accounts and can fill them in automatically. They are available as apps on phones and computers and as browser extensions.

Master password

The single password that unlocks a password manager. Everything inside the vault is encrypted with it, which means that without the master password, the vault is unreadable. This is intentional for security, but it creates a planning problem: if you are the only person who knows your master password, no one can access your other passwords after you are gone. Chapter 3 covers how to address this without compromising your security while you are alive.

Legacy Contact

A person you designate in advance to manage certain aspects of your account after your death. Apple and Facebook both use this term for their respective tools. A Legacy Contact does not receive your login credentials and typically cannot access private messages or financial information. What they can do varies by platform, but generally includes managing your memorialized profile or downloading certain data you have authorized them to receive.

Inactive Account Manager

Google's tool for deciding what happens to your Google account and data if you stop using it for a period of time you specify. You can choose to have your data deleted, share it with trusted contacts you designate, or send an automated message. It is one of the more thoughtfully designed legacy tools any major platform offers, and it is available through your Google Account settings at no cost.

Payable-on-death (POD) designation

A beneficiary instruction attached directly to a financial account that transfers the account's assets to a named person upon your death, without requiring probate. Many bank accounts, brokerage accounts, and retirement accounts allow POD designations. They are separate from your will and generally override it, which means they need to be reviewed and kept current as your wishes and relationships change. Chapter 6 covers POD designations in the context of digital financial accounts.

Seed phrase

A sequence of words, typically twelve to twenty-four, that serves as the master recovery key for a cryptocurrency wallet. If you hold cryptocurrency, your seed phrase is the only way to recover your holdings if you lose access to your wallet. There is no customer service to call and no reset option. Whoever holds the seed phrase controls the funds, which makes it among the most critical pieces of information to store securely and pass on to a trusted person through your digital estate plan.

Passkey

A newer type of login credential that replaces a traditional password with a cryptographic key stored on your device. When you log in, your phone or computer confirms your identity using biometrics like a fingerprint or face scan, and the key does the rest. Passkeys are more secure than passwords and harder to steal, but they also create an estate planning challenge: because they are tied to a specific device, a family member cannot use them to log in on their own device without additional steps. As passkeys become more common, they will require their own planning consideration.

ABOUT THE AUTHOR

Paul Wilczynski is a retired software developer whose decades of solving complex problems now fuel his work helping older adults navigate modern life. As TheSeniorTechie, he runs TheSeniorTechie.com, a site, newsletter, and workshop series created "by a senior, for seniors." In his mid-70s and living in Asheville, North Carolina, with his wife, Joan Brasier, Paul writes to spare families the avoidable digital mess he's seen too often.

ABOUT THE DESIGNER

Andrea Kulish Wilhelm is an artist, graphic designer, and pysanky teacher with a studio/gallery located in Asheville, North Carolina's River Arts District. A first-generation Ukrainian American, she learned the traditional folk art of making pysanky eggs from her mother when she was only five. When she isn't bringing pages to life with her love for books and typography, she is busy spreading joy through her art. You can check out her work at Studio A or visit ashevillestudioa.com.

ABOUT THE TYPE

The main text is typeset in Plantin MT Pro, an old-style serif typeface. It was created in 1913 by the British Monotype Corporation for their hot metal typesetting system and is named after the sixteenth-century printer Christophe Plantin.

The secondary typeface is Avenir, which is a geometric sans-serif typeface designed by Adrian Frutiger in 1987. The word avenir is French for 'future'. As the name suggests, the family takes inspiration from the geometric style of sans-serif typeface developed in the 1920s that took the circle as a basis, such as Erbar and Futura.

www.ingramcontent.com/pod-product-compliance
Lightning Source LLC
LaVergne TN
LVHW100316210926
848480LV00003B/1150